HORSE TRAINING BASICS

An Indispensable Guide for
BEGINNING TRAINERS

Deborah M. Britt

P.O. Box 7027 • Loveland, CO 80537
Alpine Publications Inc.

Horse Training Basics–An Indispensable Guide for Beginning Trainers

ISBN # 0-931866-63-4

Library of Congress Cataloging-in-Publication Data

Britt, Deborah M., 1965–
    Horse training basics : an indispensable guide for beginning
trainers / Deborah M. Britt.
        p.   cm.
    Includes bibliographical references (p.   ) and index.
    ISBN 0-931866-63-4
    1. Horses–Training. I. Title.
SF287.B82   1994
636.1′088–dc20   93-32526
                                                       CIP

1 2 3 4 5 6 7 8 9 0

Photographs by Randy Williams
Layout by Shadow Canyon Graphics

Printed in the United States of America.

Contents

Contents

To my husband, Mark Hay; my Jack Russell Terrier, Annie; and my horses, Razzle Dazzle Bay, TT Red Hot, and TW Bay Flame, who put up with me through writing, photo taking, and having their patience tested innumerable times. I love you all.

Acknowledgements

I am greatly indebted to the following people for their help and support—it was invaluable to me in creating and delivering this book: Dianne Borneman of Shadow Canyon Graphics; Stella Brown; Sheri Forsythe; Dwight and Cindy Greene of Sycamore Canyon Stables; Betty Jo McKinney of Alpine Publications, Inc.; Dr. Sandra Singleton; Randy Williams; Amy Ulovec; Matthew Vanderbilt; and all of my valued clients.

—Deborah Britt

Introduction

Owners and amateurs make up a large percentage of those who ride throughout the United States today. Many of these owners also show their horses, while others are content to enjoy their mounts in a natural setting at home or on the trail. Some of these horses are highly trained athletes, while others are family pets and babysitters. Still others are used for the handicapped, providing incomparable joy to all who work with them.

Whatever the purpose, the proper training of a horse can make a monumental difference in the amount of enjoyment and quality of time spent with the animal. The easier your horse is to handle on the ground, the more time you can spend enjoying your ride. You may be surprised at how much your horse can learn, and you may surprise yourself at how much you can teach him. With the right information and an intermediate background in horse handling, you can train your own horse in most of the basics of hauling, clipping, lunging, and riding.

It is important to look at many factors when training your young horse or retraining your older horse. Temperament, previous handling, and natural instincts all play a large part in your horse's ability and desire to learn and understand. Once you realize the influence of these factors, you will be able to use them to your benefit and make training that much easier.

Respect plays an equally important role. Without mutual respect, your horse may react out of fear or may attempt to escape from pain instead of performing out of a desire to please. While this may be effective temporarily, the key to successful training lies in your ability to nurture trust and respect in your horse and to take the time and patience to teach rather than bully. In return, your horse will learn and perform willingly and will become a loyal member of your family.

I "retired" from horse training at the age of twenty-one because I was tired of the weekly shows and the large show string, all of which left me little bonding time with each animal and no pleasure time for my own horses. After three years, I was convinced to return to training by people at the stable who owned horses that had been abused in the past or trained improperly. At first they wanted suggestions on how to "fix" these horses, but it soon became evident that a lot of abuse was occurring and that far too many horses were becoming casualties of the "ninety-day-wonder" philosophy on training.

I began training again with a different frame of mind. I wanted to help these horses that had become social outcasts to regain the potential that they had been born with, and I wanted their owners to know that, with the right training, they could work with their own horses without "ruining" any previous training. More than anything, I wanted to reform horses that had a negative past and return them as functional members into an environment where they could work and prosper without fear or abuse. Many of these horses have gone on to successful show careers, a possibility that had never entered their owners' minds. Most people do not realize that behavioral problems are usually created by improper handling and training rather than by the natural temperament of the horse.

My goal in writing this book is to help you create your own talented equine friend. I am assuming that you, as a handler, have had solid experience with horses in the past and are ready to take the step from rider to teacher. You should attempt the concepts presented in this book only if you have ridden for several years, have handled a few difficult animals, and basically understand the psyche of the horse. If you haven't had enough experience, don't fret. There will come a day when you know that you have put in enough hours to try training on your own. When you do, this book will give you the know-how to accomplish it. In the meantime, it will give you solid basics and a goal to work toward.

Horse Training Basics will take you step by step through proven training techniques and allow you to train your own horse to lunge, clip, and load and to learn many other useful ground manners. The illustrations will show you exactly how to perform a given procedure. You will also learn how to desensitize your horse to normal sights and sensations—a technique that will make breaking and handling much easier. You will gain insight into your horse's mind and perceptions, which will allow you to see that much of his behavior is affected by things beyond your control, but not beyond your influence.

For ease of reading, "he" is used throughout the book to describe the horse. This is in no way meant to eliminate the female gender, nor does it imply that the techniques are any less effective on mares than on stallions or geldings.

Whether you have been riding the same horse for years or are a recent owner of a new horse, this book will save you invaluable time and the frustration of training your horse by trial and error. It will let you know what *you* can teach your horse and when you should turn to a professional. It will teach you humane ways of disciplining your horse and help you to understand him and his actions. It will give you the knowledge and encouragement you need to teach your own horse from the ground up, to develop a strong bond based on mutual respect and admiration, and to mold your horse into a pleasurable companion. Enough talk—let's get to work!

The Right Horse

Getting what you want from your horse depends upon many factors. You must, first and foremost, have the right horse for the type of work or pleasure you intend. Second, you need to establish a trusting relationship with the horse. Finally, he must be adequately trained.

If your riding experience is limited, don't start out with a young, untrained horse. An older, broke horse will bring maturity to the relationship and any training will be minimal. He will normally be less explosive and will already know most of the basics. He has experienced various sights, sounds, smells, and situations and will know how to act under a given set of circumstances. Your venture into training can reasonably start with reinforcing his ground manners, training him some new behaviors that he has not previously mastered, and perfecting his performance for the show ring or trail.

If you have been riding and handling horses for a number of years and have a good understanding of horse behavior, know how to "read" a horse's body language, and feel comfortable with various methods of discipline, you may be ready to take on a green horse, retrain an older horse that has a few problems, or start a young colt or filly. As a beginning trainer, be cautious. Never take on a horse that you know is beyond your ability to handle. If a horse you own is giving

1

you problems that you are unable to correct, seek help from a professional trainer. And never be ashamed to ask for help or advice when you run into a particularly difficult situation. You can't learn horse training overnight—it takes patience, experience, and years of working around horses to become a good trainer. Most of all, it takes a great deal of time and a commitment to consistent daily lessons. Nevertheless, you may find it very fulfilling to teach your horse good manners and do his basic schooling yourself. Understanding the basics of training will also make you a better handler, and give you added skill in coping with problems that may arise with your trained horse.

You need to determine and weigh several important factors before you know if a horse is right for the use and training you plan. Just because a horse is attractive, available, or has a reasonable price tag does not mean he will satisfy your needs and lead to a pleasurable riding experience. You must know what you want the horse to do, how old you want the horse to be, and what personality works best with you and other family members who may work with the horse.

If you are planning to purchase a horse to train, many important considerations enter into the decision making process. We will examine these in the rest of this chapter. If you already have a horse that fits your needs and are eager to get on with his training, please skip over to Chapter 2.

What's Your Line?

Your choice of horse will depend greatly on your purpose. Sit down early and outline exactly what you expect this horse to do. If you plan on showing him, will he be shown English or western? If he will be shown English, will you ride huntseat, saddleseat, or dressage? Do you want to eventually drive your horse? Will you want to advance to working over fences? If you decide to ride western, will you show in pleasure classes, or will you gear more toward gaming and gymkhana? Does working cattle interest you? How about pattern classes such as trail or reining?

If you are looking for a trail horse, will you be the only one riding the horse? Should the horse be able to be handled by anyone other than yourself? Is someone large or heavy going to ride your horse? Are children going to be riding out on trail? Will you be going on long, tiring rides, or is a quiet ride in the country more your style? Do you want a horse that will be a challenge, or would you rather relax and let your mind wander on your rides? As you can see, the factors to be considered are innumerable. Choose the important ones and make sure that the horse you are interested in will be able to accommodate them.

After you have determined your ideal physical and personality type, evaluate the horse that you are considering to see if he will be capable of living up to your expectations. When you look at a horse, go over your checklist in your mind and apply each answer to the horse. Look beyond the physical appearance of the horse and evaluate his mental and structural potential.

Keep in mind that nothing in horses is for certain. You may purchase a horse that seems to have all of the qualifications that you desire only to find out three months down the road that you were wrong and the horse is otherwise predispositioned. If this is the case, you must determine if you want to change your expectations and utilize the horse's strengths by going on a different track, or if you should sell this horse and find one that will be suited for your original purpose. The decision is yours alone to make, but give it careful thought before taking action. Sometimes you will need to be flexible and re-evaluate your plans.

You may also find that your horse is capable of crossing class lines where you never imagined he would. Take for instance a horse that has been purchased to show western in your local shows. One day out on the trail, you find that your western horse has an incredible ground-covering trot. After testing this possibility, you find that when

he is in the right frame, he can open up and trot with the best of
them. You may well be on your way to discovering that this horse
can do *both* western and hunter. Explore your options with your horse
and you may discover other enjoyable aspects of performance.

Let's Get Physical

Leg soundness on any horse being considered for purchase should
be a prime concern. Many problems that occur later in life begin earlier
than age six and are recognizable through veterinarian X-rays. Beyond
this, most leg problems can be detected through professional observa-
tion, palpitation, and nerve blocking of the leg. If any major indicator
is revealed, do not purchase the horse. It is not worth the risk. Nine
times out of ten, the horse will go lame on you, and all of your money
and training will be for naught.

When you first examine the leg, look for the straightness of the
horse's track and the squareness of the stance. The horse's front and
rear legs should be parallel, and the toes of the hooves should point
forward. The horse's feet should appear large and round. He should
have strong, healthy heels and a hoof size large enough to accommodate his size and weight. When the horse walks, his hind feet should
track on the same line as his front feet. Notice the length and freedom
of the stride. The horse should show reach without hitching or
appearing uncomfortable in any way. Any deviation is cause for
further evaluation. The horse should step firmly on all four feet. View
any signs of favoring as a red flag to future problems.

After observing the horse, run your hands slowly and deliberately
down each leg. Use your fingertips to probe the joints, muscles, and
tendons of the leg, noticing any heat, swelling, hardening, or tender-
ness. If any is found, go back to the area and explore more closely.
You may find signs of a previous bowed tendon or splint.

Notice also the horse's reaction to your examination. Does he
stand quietly, or is he uncomfortable and trying to move around? This

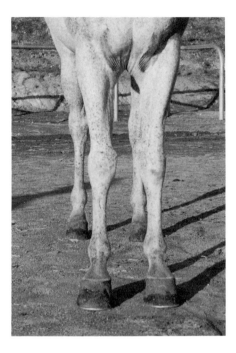

Proper alignment for front and back legs with all feet and legs appearing square and straight.

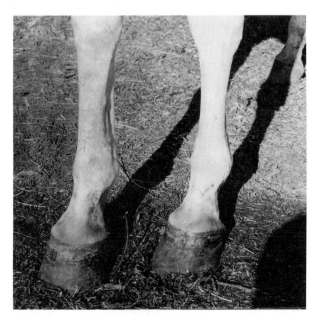

The lump on this horse's right front leg, half way between knee and fetlock, is a splint. It is actually a small fracture of the bone.

will give you an indication as to how much the horse has been handled, and if the horse has had extensive vet work. If the horse becomes leery and upset the moment you start to act like a veterinarian, he probably has had significant exposure to the vet, and this could mean a past medical history. It is worth checking out.

If you feel a definite separation in the tendon and the bone, or if one area of the tendon is larger on one leg than on another, chances are this horse has had a bowed tendon in the past. While a bowed tendon can heal fairly normally, this horse has had permanent damage to the tendon of that leg and will be susceptible to lameness later in life. His legs may last a year or ten years, but either way, it is not worth the risk. If you suspect tendon damage and you plan on using the horse regularly, pass on this particular horse.

Splints can also be determined through palpitation. If you feel a hard lump on any of the legs, it is most likely a splint. Before ruling the horse out, however, watch him in motion. If he is sound at all gaits (including an extended trot) and no heat is present, he has probably healed completely and the splint should not pose a problem in the future. You may, however, want to consider the horse's chance of reinjuring himself in the same way. If the horse has front legs that are close set, if he toes-in with the front legs, or if he has a tendency to overreach, interference may become a constant problem.

Many leg problems can be determined only by an X-ray. The methods just discussed will help you to rule out any obvious problems, but if you have taken all precautions and feel that this horse is for you, have a veterinarian check the horse completely before you spend a lot of money to purchase the horse. Request that the veterinarian do a thorough physical and leg X-rays on the horse. Also ask the owner to provide any vet records they have available. A few dollars and a little extra attention now can prevent you from immeasurable heartache in the future.

A horse's topline is also an important consideration in the future use of the horse. Adhere strictly to any breed specifications if you are purchasing an animal for reproduction. In general, if the horse is to be used for performance, look for a slight slope from the point of the croup (the highest part of the horse's rump) to the tail. This will allow the horse to drop his hind end and get under himself, creating drive and impulsion.

Various breeds have different tendencies regarding the slope of the croup. Most Quarter Horses show a significant slope, whereas Arabians are bred to be quite flat across the croup. This reflects the intended purpose of the horse. But don't be fooled by comparing one breed to another. Many times, the actual angle of the bone is the same but the muscling is different, which means that an Arabian with a slight slope may be able to get under himself as well as a Quarter Horse that has a more pronounced slope. If you are in doubt, get the breed specifications and compare the horse to the breed ideal. Unless the horse has hip or stifle problems or an extremely short croup and only slight angles through the hocks, he will be able to use his hind end properly.

Build is another consideration when evaluating your future companion. Common sense should take precedence here, and an eye toward beauty should not lend a deaf ear toward build and practicality. If you are a larger person, look for a horse that will accommodate your height and weight. An 800-pound horse is obviously not suitable for a 170-pound man. If you are going to be roping cattle, don't get a fine-boned horse that is going to be jerked around and injured by a sizable calf. If you are going to be riding saddleseat, don't look for a stock-type horse with a low neck set. You get the idea. Evaluate your needs and choose a horse accordingly. It will prevent frustration later.

The topic of shoulder slopes in performance horses is often discussed as if it were a religion. Some experts feel that the slope of the shoulder is the distinguishing characteristic between a mediocre horse and an exceptional one. Others feel that it is a load of hogwash and that if the horse can move properly, that is all that matters. Realistically, both ideas share valid points. Unless you plan on training a high-performance, highly motioned English or driving horse, shoulder angle should not be your *main* concern. If should, however, enter the picture if your horse will be used for breeding or showing, and it should be analyzed before you purchase the horse. It is important that the slope and length of the shoulder be properly proportioned to allow freedom of movement and length of stride.

A horse in either of these categories should have a long, well-laid-back shoulder that allows freedom of the leg and chest so that the horse can perform in the manner in which he is presented. If you have a western pleasure horse, you can get away with a shoulder slope that is a little straighter than ideal. If the horse will be used for roping, cutting, or any extreme physical work, however, too straight of a shoulder will be a definite hindrance. If you are training a dressage horse, an English pleasure horse, or a hunter, you will look for a long, sloping shoulder that is slightly prominent in the chest area and that is well set into the girth area. You should be able to put your fist between the girth and the point of elbow. This configuration allows the horse maximum mobility and reach in the front end, which is necessary for the high-performance horse to function properly and efficiently.

While you are examining the shoulder, also notice the angle at which the horse's neck is set into the shoulder and withers. For the horse that is used strictly for pleasure, neck set may be only as important as the preference of the rider. For the show horse, neck set may very well determine the function and capability of the horse. If you want a horse that will be shown western or huntseat, look for one that has his neck set low on the shoulder, but not so low that it restricts mobility. This is also true for working cow horses. This conformation allows the horse to drop down from the withers into the bridle with his head closer to the ground. While working cattle, the horse can watch what is happening with the cow or calf and act accordingly. This neck set also protects the rider from injury because it reduces the

Note the long, laid back slope of the shoulder and the high set of the neck. This horse is built for English or driving performance where the set of the neck should be high.

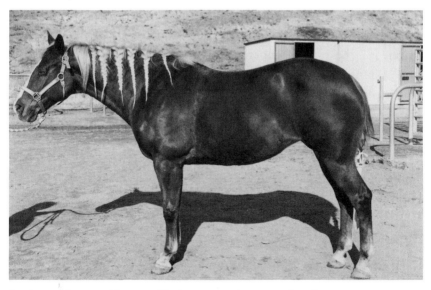

Stock type horse with naturally low set neck appropriate for western or hunter pleasure.

tendency of the horse to throw his head up and hit the rider in the face. The western or hunter horse is judged on his ease and way of going, and this lower head set gives the horse a pleasant, unhurried appearance.

If the horse will be used for saddleseat, driving, or dressage, the desired neck set is much higher. These horses are required to perform with maximum loft and elevation while exhibiting an air of elegance and grace. A horse that has a lower neck set is more likely to carry his weight low and in the front end. A horse that is set higher will be able to shift his weight and center of gravity slightly backward, freeing his front end for elevation. Once again, purpose determines build. Decide what you want before you go out looking.

Which Breed?

Not only do breeds determine the genetic build of the horse, they dispose temperament as well. While no rule holds true one hundred percent of the time, tendencies can be expected and utilized in your search for the right companion. Within every breed you will also find individual differences in temperament and personality, and these traits, plus the horse's soundness, are extremely important when choosing the right horse. The observations noted here are generalities regarding the different breeds. Remember that each horse should be evaluated on his own merits and drawbacks. Additionally, no two horses of any breed are exactly alike, and don't forget—there are exceptions to every rule. With that said, here are a few of the most common breeds and what they may be most suited for.

Appaloosa

The Appaloosa began on the plains with a mixture of wild, domestic, and foreign blood. It was treasured for its wide variety of colors and markings. Indeed, a strikingly marked Appaloosa will catch almost anyone's eye. It was also known for its sprint speeds and agility across the rolling plains.

The Appaloosa is well suited for serious work due to its being a combination of stock and wild breeds. Its build makes this horse perfect for trail riding or the show ring, and its variety allows it to be suited to almost any size of person. An Appaloosa can sometimes be tricky to handle, but for the experienced horseman, the challenge may be fun. This horse is very loyal and is rarely afraid to tackle trails, cows, and the like. The Appaloosa's coloring also makes it ideal for parades, costumes, and any event where you wish to be noticed.

American Saddlebred

The Saddlebred has often been touted as one of the proudest breeds alive. Indeed, its lofty carriage and extreme motion make it the perfect horse to be shown under saddle or harness. Because of its flash and manner, this breed is difficult to ignore in the show ring. The size of the breed makes this horse ideal for adult and child alike, and you will rarely find a Saddlebred without an amusing personality.

The Saddlebred's usefulness is not limited to the show ring. Many pleasure-driving horses have been crossed with Saddlebreds to refine the larger-boned animals and give them a style and class of their own. The trained Saddlebred can also be a wonderful companion for younger members of the family, and its sense of humor will endear the horse to almost everyone. Because of the Saddlebred's temperament and mind set, this horse is rarely adverse to doing the repetitive work necessary for equitation patterns and is often an exciting junior show mount. Trail is also not out of the Saddlebred's realm. If properly shod, and if the horse possesses a calm temperament, the Saddlebred can be a pleasant ride out in the wilderness, although you better make sure that his head doesn't get in the way when ducking branches!

Arabian

The Arabian is one of the most beautiful and intelligent of the breeds. It was bred in the deserts for stamina, strength, beauty, and loyalty, and most of these basic components carry forth to the Arabians of today. More than once, these horses have been referred to as living works of art, and their vitality and presence make them a favorite to watch. Unfortunately, the Arabian has also gained a reputation for being difficult to handle. It is interesting to note that the Arabian is one of only two breeds that allow stallions to be shown by junior riders. While many Arabians are extremely easy to work with, the reputation that many Arabians have achieved is not solely the responsibility of a misinformed public. Arabians do have a tendency to be a little more difficult to handle at times, partly due to their high intelligence. It is unfortunate, but common, for beginning riders and owners to be drawn to the horse by its beauty, only to find that they are overmatched in the training department. Because of this dilemma, there are many high-strung and spoiled Arabians on the market, and many people are unprepared to deal with this problem.

The flip side of the coin is this: With proper handling and training, the Arabian can become one of your most devoted companions. The breed has a high stamina factor and usually will give 100 percent to the task at hand. These horses are quick to solve problems and learn at a remarkable pace. It is unfortunate that many Arabians are not suited for larger people, although at times you can find large Arabians. In fact, many of the crosses today lend themselves to a taller, bigger-bodied animal.

The Arabian that has been properly handled will do very well both on the trail and in the show ring. Its natural beauty is eye catching, and its carriage and elegance allow the horse to be noticed easily. The Arabian has a higher lung capacity and larger nasal-passage openings than many of the breeds, making the breed ideal for strenuous distance riding and for tackling rough terrains. The breed is quick and sure-footed—another asset on the trail—and, if properly conditioned, will not tire easily. If you like some spark and have handled horses before, you may be attracted to the Arabian.

Paints

The Paint horse combines the beauty of color and the practicality of the Quarter Horse and was bred to take advantage of both. Like the Appaloosa, the Paint is treasured for its eye-catching color and solid build. Because this breed is of stock type, the Paint can be used for working almost any type of livestock as well as for performing in the show ring.

Because of its coloring, the Paint is often seen in parades and show rings across the nation. The breed's genealogy makes this horse quiet and even tempered—ideally suited for the junior exhibitor. Its build makes the breed perfect for cow work, stock and reining, and western and hunter pleasure. The Paint horse is also at home on the trail, combining athletic ability with common sense and a level head. Being of stock descent, the Paint is usually tall and full bodied, making this horse suitable for even the largest of men. To combine the beauty of color with the practicality of size, choose a Paint.

Quarter Horse

The Quarter Horse has long been a favorite of the cowboy and exhibitor alike. Its size and bulk make this horse ideal for any strain of working competition, especially when it involves working stock. This breed is also physically suited for almost any size and weight of rider. Trail is often one of this horse's favorite pastimes, because he can relax and enjoy what is occurring around him.

Most known for a quiet temperament and an easy gait, the older Quarter Horse is the perfect companion for most beginning riders.

This is the horse that can teach children and fearful adults to enjoy riding. A well-trained Quarter Horse is a delight on the trail and can come back in and work cattle without ever breaking stride. This horse possesses the beauty of function and form and often becomes a rider's best friend. If you are just starting out, try to find a seasoned Quarter Horse that can help teach you to ride.

Tennessee Walkers and Other Gaited Horses

There is a reason why many riding tours and trail strings are switching to gaited horses—they are a delight to ride. You don't have to worry about bouncing around at the trot or getting jarred out of the saddle. For trail riding, the gaited horses are the Cadillacs of the horse world.

While not always the most eye catching, the gaited horse has a beauty all his own. He seems to float across the ground, and while you are on his back, you will begin to believe that it is true. Most Walkers are gentle by nature, and if you look, you can find one to fit almost any size. The Tennessee Walker is slightly limited in the show ring in that the breed is not trained to trot. Gaited classes are also difficult to find. The ignorance of many judges hinders the proper evaluation of the gaited horse. Nonetheless, if you are persistent, you will find that a gaited horse is as well suited for the ring as it is for the trail. If you want the benefits of an easy chair and a trail ride, you may want to look into purchasing a gaited horse.

These are the practical issues involved in looking for a horse. What about the emotional side? What happens if your daughter falls in love with a particular horse and doesn't care if he has three eyes and five legs? By discussing the criteria ahead of time with all parties involved, you may be able to head off some of these problems. Let all individuals who will be involved with the horse help determine the purpose and intent of owning the horse. Work out differences as much as possible before you start shopping. If you want a bay and your spouse wants a gray, who will win? It sounds silly, but sometimes it comes down to that.

Emotions and gut instinct play an important role in choosing a horse, but keep them in check by being realistic about your purpose. Decide what you want, then allow your emotions to determine which horse will be best for you *within your given guidelines.* Who knows? You may find a chestnut gelding that fits all the important criteria, when all along you were looking for a bay mare. Keep important criteria in mind and be flexible on the little items. Doing this and paying attention to your first impressions will no doubt stand you well in your equine search.

It is very important that you be aware of your own personality and expectations when you look at any horse of any breed. If you know that you are a little timid, and if you want an easy, reliable ride—even if you have been riding for years—a Saddlebred may be too much for you. Perhaps you should gear your efforts toward finding a well-broke Paint or Quarter Horse. If you like a challenge and are looking for a horse that will keep you on your toes, you may want to purchase an Arabian. Whichever way you go, you need to determine clearly what personality will work best with you and the purpose for which you intend to use the horse. All other decisions should be worked around that basic premise.

Now that you have determined exactly what it is that you seek, start shopping. Don't be afraid to visit many farms or ranches to get an idea of your personal preference concerning height, gender, color, and size. Look through your local horse-industry paper to get a feel for prices and for what is available in your marketplace. Good horses can be found from someone's backyard as well as from a huge ranch. See as many horses as you can, and do not get too hung up on one horse until all inspections and vet checks have been done and passed. Usually, your first instinct will be a good one. Barring any unforeseen circumstances such as bone spurs or chronic lameness, the horse will probably be a good match for you. If you feel good about him after handling him and riding him, have a vet check. If you are hesitant, look elsewhere. When you find the right horse for you, you will feel it. If he passes your vet check, buy him.

When comparing young horses to older horses, keep in mind that the personality of the horse will change as he gets older. A flighty two-year-old will likely turn out to be a nice horse once he gets some age and maturity on his side. The older horse will tend to get more docile as he ages. This, of course, does not hold true for each and every horse. In fact, a few become even grumpier in their old age. These are only guidelines on what is *likely* to occur, not necessarily what *will* occur.

If you find a young horse that seems to have a lot of potential and you have worked extensively with horses in the past, do not avoid a purchase just because he seems a little energetic or high-strung. This may be a result of youth and nothing more. This is not to suggest, however, that you go out and buy a baby if you are in-experienced. Too many things can go wrong with inexperience on both sides, and both will end up unhappy. As a rule of thumb, an inexperienced horseman should stick to a more mature, trained horse —at least until he is comfortable working with horses and has a solid grasp of the basics of horse mentality and horsemanship. Indeed, no one should attempt to train a horse until he is comfortable with his own skills and experience and has been riding and working around horses for some time.

Never buy a broke horse until you have ridden him and, better yet, until several people in your family have ridden him. A horse that seems quiet and mannerly on the ground may have had very little training under saddle. Habits and vices are more easily recognizable when you are sitting on the horse's back.

Unless you plan to take the horse straight to a trainer, consider the amount of training that the horse already has gained. If the horse does not respond to even the most basic of commands, you must decide if you want to put months of training into the horse. If you do, you need to decide if you are truly capable of doing such extensive training or if you wll need to enlist the help of a trainer. There are too many nice horses out there to settle for one that will cause you heartache in the future. Keep looking until you find what you really want.

Unless you have prior experience in training, do not purchase a horse that bucks, rears, bolts, spins, or otherwise lets you know that you are not welcome as a passenger. These are problems that should be handled only by the experienced horseman. Attempting to do so without proper training may result in serious injury. These horses have been mishandled in the past either through improper training or lack of training, and extensive work will be required to correct these behaviors. Most of these horses must be taken back to the basics and reworked until they can be ridden. It takes time, energy, skill, and patience to reform this type of horse. If this is what you want, fine. If not, look elsewhere for your mount.

One of the greatest fears of many owners is ending up with a horse that is a living demon. Some problem horses are difficult to spot when you spend such a brief time with them before purchase. The best solution is to convince the current owner to allow you to take the horse for a specific time to "try him out" and see if he fits your needs. This is common in show barns but may be difficult between personal parties. The best situation, if possible, is to draw up a contract between both parties that protects the interest of the owner yet allows you the flexibility of a trial run. If the owners are dead set against it, return at a different time and ride the horse again. The more time you spend on his back, the greater chance you have of spotting any problems.

Don't be afraid to ask the owner for veterinary and shot records, show records, and a brief history of the horse. You won't always get the whole story, but it can't hurt to ask. Many owners will be up front enough to tell you about past problems and how they worked through them or about personality traits that may affect your decision.

If they offer only praises of the horse, take their words with a grain of salt. No horse is perfect, and, just like a person, he will have his good and bad points. Let your instincts guide you when you decide what to believe and what not to believe.

When you ride the horse, try to notice subtle signs that will tell you how he is feeling. While you can't expect a horse that you have never ridden to respond immediately to your cues and way of riding, you *can* expect him to understand the basics. If a horse is hesitant to bend one way, ask him again. If he becomes increasingly reluctant, he is telling you that there is a problem. It may be something as simple as muscle stiffness or as complicated as a structural flaw. Notice the horse's moods and attitudes as you work through different maneuvers. Is the horse happy and trying to please, or is he resentful and uncomfortable? Examine all inconsistencies until you are satisfied with the answers. After all, you are the one paying for the horse, and you are the one who has to live with your decision.

Talking to others who know the horse can also be a great source of information. Don't be afraid to ask who the owner uses as a vet or trainer. If you are truly interested in the horse, call these people and ask their opinions. Most of the time, you will receive up-front, honest answers. You will also want to talk to anyone who has ridden with or shown against the horse. They may be able to tell you about positive or negative behaviors that they have observed.

The importance of a thorough check by a competent veterinarian cannot be stressed enough. Find your own vet. Do not rely on the one who has previously worked on the horse. Your vet may find something that the other vet has missed, and you will be assured of an outside, objective opinion. If you have any doubts, err on the side of being overly cautious. The old saying holds true—it's better to be safe than sorry.

To Be or Not To Be

Congratulations. You have lived through the headache of buying a horse. Now what? First of all, be realistic. Over the next few weeks, you will begin to know and understand your new horse. You will discover his habits, his personality, his likes, and his dislikes, and you will gain some inkling of his disposition. As you begin working under saddle, you will get an idea whether he will live up to your hopes and expectations. Realize that you cannot accomplish everything at once. Take one day at a time and evaluate your horse's progress. Some training may be glaringly lacking and difficult to teach, while you may be surprised at his understanding and grasp of other training concepts. Intensive training takes time, and it helps to keep in mind that no training is ever totally complete.

As you get to know your horse, evaluate his capabilities and how they might fit into your plans. If he needs more training than you thought, be patient and put in the necessary time to help him reach those goals. Rushing a horse can be a big mistake, and you may find yourself months later starting at square one. Approach every day of training with realism and tempered hopes. A champion is not made overnight, and lifetime bonds are not built in a day.

Continue to evaluate your horse's progress, because this is as important as appraising your original goals. When you purchased the horse, you had an idea of how long you thought it might take to form the friend that you wanted. Those time frames could have been anything from immediately to years down the road. As you begin to understand your horse, compare these original time estimates with your current ones. Are you still on track, or will the training take more or less time than you anticipated? Do you feel that your horse is still suited for the purpose that you originally intended, or should you explore other avenues? Constant reevaluation will allow you to direct your horse's training in the most effective and efficient manner.

What if you find that your horse isn't capable of the tasks for which he was purchased? Do you give up? The answer to that question is largely a personal one, but if you decide to hang in there, at least for a while, how do you determine where to go next? The answer is to go back to the basics. Evaluate your horse with an impartial eye and ask yourself, with your newly gained knowledge, what is this horse good for? The answer will probably be staring you right in the face. Look at your horse's attributes and the gaits with which he is most comfortable, then decide from there. A quiet, mellow horse will never be a high-powered English horse, so why not try him western? Look for disciplines that suit your horse's personality. If your horse has shown interest in livestock in the past, try working cattle with him. You will be amazed at how obvious his use is once you find the right persuasion.

This entire process of discovery and rediscovery takes time and patience. Your initial impressions may have been right, and you may have exactly the horse that you wanted. If this is the case, good for you. If not, don't give up hope. Just like every person, every horse has his calling. You just need to find out what it is and if you want to join him in that pursuit. Unless you are pressed for time, you may actually find this process exciting. It's like opening a Christmas present—you never know what you will find until you get inside.

Getting To Know
Each Other

Training your horse occurs on several levels. Physical, mental, and emotional factors all influence the amount of success or failure that you achieve. It is crucial that no avenue be left unaddressed and that no level be left untrained, for it is *that one thing* that will come back to haunt you in the future.

When you start working with a new horse, you are a stranger to him. He has no reason to respect, trust, or even like you. Your first goal is to establish a relationship with him, one that hopefully will grow to a long and fruitful friendship. Ideally, you should spend at least an hour a day for the first week or so talking, petting, and establishing the groundwork for future training.

It is important to create a strong relationship with your horse before training commences. You need to spend time "just hanging out" with your horse, allowing him to become familiar with the sound of your voice and the feel of your touch. It is a little easier to accomplish this with a horse if he is somewhat isolated from other horses, such as in a pipe corral or box stall. If your only accommodation is a pasture with other horses, you can still achieve the same results, but the process will take slightly longer.

It is important to allow much of the first free contact to come from the horse. Lower yourself closer to the ground, placing yourself in a less threatening position. This will encourage the horse's curiosity.

When you first put your horse into new surroundings, stay with him. While you may not be his closest friend right now, you are still a constant that will help him in the following days and weeks. You are the only constant left over from his previous environment, although your earlier contact may have been brief. Allow him to explore his new home and, in the process, explore and bond with you. All you need to do is sit in a nonthreatening position and watch. If he comes over to you, pet his nose and chest and talk to him, but allow him to continue exploring independently.

By starting out this way, you will teach your horse that he has some rights in this relationship. You are showing a willingness to proceed slowly rather than forcing your will immediately upon the animal. Continuing this approach during training will promote trust versus fear as a motivator, and you will accomplish much more in a shorter amount of time. You will also force yourself into a teaching and understanding role rather than into the role of enforcer. This differentiation will become increasingly important as training proceeds.

Imprinting is a recent development in training, and although it is still being studied, it may have some benefit in introducing yourself to your horse. Imprinting involves gently blowing into your horse's nose to allow him to distinguish your scent from that of other handlers. Letting him smell your hands and clothes will also help him to form a bond with you. Make eye contact with your horse, and always do plenty of talking to soothe and comfort him. He will become accustomed to your voice and will listen for it to provide direction in a time of panic.

My Space, Your Space

You've been told all your life that every man's home is his castle. A horse feels the same way. Actually, a horse's corral or stall is considered by him to be his domain. This is where he eats, sleeps, and has established whatever hierarchy is necessary to maintain peace in his surroundings. Now, all of a sudden, you come along. You have either moved him into a totally foreign environment or you have changed the major influences in his life. An adjustment period will follow. It is in your best interest to be sensitive to those changes and to allow him a period of adjustment for him to get comfortable again.

From this day forward, this is his home and you are the guest. The first rule of horse training is *never to train a horse in his stall or corral.* This is his sanctuary, and if you have any hope of building a solid relationship with him, you will allow this area to be his refuge. This does not mean that rules shouldn't be enforced in the corral (such as no biting or kicking), only that actual training should be done out-side in an arena, an enclosed area, or a tie rack.

Along with his sense of home, a horse develops a "comfort zone" at a young age. The comfort zone extends three to four feet around the horse and is considered by him to be his area. The zone acts pri-marily as a protection against the aggressive advances of other horses, and it serves to define the horse's personal space. It is important to keep this in mind at this stage of training. While you are leading and grooming your horse, he may be acutely aware of his own space but be totally oblivious to yours. He may also regard you as an intruder in his area. When this happens, you will find six feet walking where only your two should be. Your horse must be taught that you also have a comfort zone of space that must be respected. You have your rights, too, and by enforcing your space at this stage of the game, you will avoid problems later. To do this, make sure that when you are leading, your horse stays to your right and is not allowed to crowd you. When you groom him, your horse must be made to pay attention to where you are and what you are doing, and to his own body, feet, and head. There is nothing worse than having a horse catch you on the side of the head with his head (which is twice as large and equally hard)! At the same time, be aware that you can crowd him and provoke a confrontation. Never make a horse feel as though he is trapped. If it comes down to you or him, chances are you will be the one to get hurt.

The goal is to train your horse to accept you as a nonthreatening entity within his space. This brings us back to the old rule of never walking up to a horse's rear without talking to him and putting a hand on his rump. It may be an old rule, but it is a good one. Your horse needs to be made overtly aware of your presence. You can't assume that somewhere in his previous training someone has taught him to respect humans. Many times this is not the case. This brings us to a new but equally important rule. Don't assume that anything has already been done with your horse. Assuming this is the surest way to get hurt. When working with a new horse, start from the beginning until you know firsthand what he has been taught and what training still needs to be done.

Communication

Talking to your horse plays an important part in all phases of training, and if you get into the habit now, it will become second nature to you. When you talk while working with your horse, he will actually begin to learn basic commands before you intentionally "teach" them. He will start to use his ears more and will listen to the sound of your voice even though he doesn't yet understand the words. Talking during routine grooming will also accustom him to the normal tone of your voice and to the difference in meaning that accompanies a change in inflection. You will learn more about how to use this technique later.

As you and your horse get to know each other, a bond will begin to form. He will learn what is expected of him, and you will learn what is expected of you. You will soon see the mood changes and personality traits that are his and his alone, and you will learn how to most effectively interact with him through these phases.

I cannot stress enough the importance of being aware around your horse. If you stay aware, he can teach you many things about himself and will give you clues as to when he is about to do something you may not like. He can also show you a rich, full personality that many times will have you falling down laughing and preparing a tape for "America's Funniest Home Videos." Allow him to develop his personality *without* allowing him to develop the habits that may follow. If you stay aware and on your toes, you will know the difference.

Building Trust

Several signs indicate that your horse is beginning to be comfortable with you and that some measure of trust is forming. The first sign to appear usually is recognition upon arrival. Your horse will lift up his head as he hears your voice and may walk toward you as you approach his gate. Any movement in your direction should be praised and reinforced. Treats work well to get this behavior started, but make sure that they are healthy, like commercial cubes, carrots or apples. Sugar cubes may taste good, but they really aren't good for the horse.

Don't "play" with your horse at this stage (chasing him off and coaxing him to come back). Instead, make every time that he sees you a positive, nonthreatening experience. It is important that you give him an environment without fear in order for learning to take place. There is plenty of time later to play or to introduce scary objects.

Because you and your horse are just now beginning to bond, focus all of his training and senses on building trust. Sight and smell will take care of themselves as long as the horse is allowed to approach you freely and check up on you periodically. Be careful not to control his curiosity. If he wants to bend around and smell your back as you groom, let him. Just make sure that you stay on your toes and don't let a nuzzle turn into a nip. You often need to work with your horse on touch and taste as recognition senses. As previously mentioned, treats will go a long way in helping you to bond with your horse. The quickest way to a horse's heart is through his stomach. Be careful, though, about overtreating your horse, because it can make him pushy and prone to nip. The rule of thumb is to lavish him a bit at the beginning, than cut down on the amount of treats. Put the treats in his feeder if you feel that a problem is beginning to arise.

You can never lavish too much grooming and touching on your horse. Horses loved to be brushed and rubbed. Invest in a good stiff brush, a medium brush, and a Grooma® (a stiff rubber curry that removes loose hair nicely and is perfect for getting at those itchy spots). Your horse will love you forever and will look forward to your grooming ritual.

When you are involved in any type of training, it is important to be aware of the *perception* of the person or animal with whom you are working. A horse is no different. Regardless of how human you think he is, the fact remains that your horse sees, hears, smells, and processes information in a different way than you do. Your horse also possesses a strong set of instincts that affects his moods, fears, and perceptions.

Let's go back for a moment and look at the evolution of the horse. The horse is, by nature, a grazing animal that relied heavily on his senses to survive the perils encountered in the wild. One of his most important senses was sight. The eyes of a horse are placed wide on the head and are pointed outward so that when the head is down for feeding, the horse is able to maintain his vigilance in front and peripherally. When the head is raised for motion, the eyes are able to focus to the front or to the side as needed. The horse cannot, however, see where his feet are stepping without lowering his head and neck. A horse prefers to place his feet on solid footing that will not give way when he turns or pushes off to move forward. The *last* place he wants to step is on something that is unreliable or unstable (such as your toes).

Because of this positioning of the eyes, a horse's depth perception is radically different from that of a human. The composition of the eye

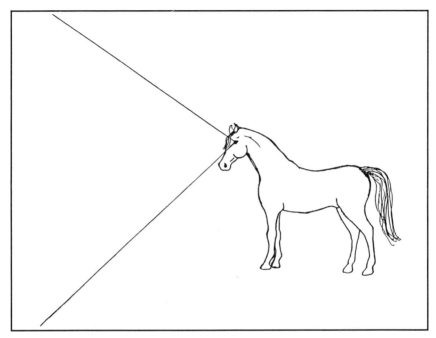

The horse's field of vision does not include the area immediately in front of his feet. In order to see objects or obstacles immediately in front of him, he must lower his head and rotate his eyes forward.

uses various shades of black and white to determine depth and distance, which makes some dark places look like holes and the calculations for jumps difficult without the inclusion of a white ground pole. This can explain why a horse may panic when asked to step into water. To him, it may look like a bottomless hole! It also explains why a horse can mistakenly step on your foot. A horse cannot see where his feet are at the time he contacts the ground, and because your foot wasn't there the last time he looked, he may inadvertently step on you. Keep this in mind when building trail or obstacle courses for your horse, and be sure to paint bridges white and include ground poles around jumps. Also, pay close attention to where you are putting your own feet. Keep them out from under your horse's feet rather than relying on him to stay off yours.

Beyond visual differences, the horse also has sensory differences. His senses of smell, sound, and movement are acute, and while you may like to think that your horse's attention is completely on you, quite the opposite is true. A horse, especially a young one, is constantly watching and evaluating his environment and processing any "bogeymen" that he might find. This explains why a youngster is particularly difficult to handle on a windy day. His senses are on overload and he sees monsters at every corner. Understanding this will make it easier for you to see the motives behind the unruliness and to be a little more patient when faced with this situation.

Instincts also play a part in the horse's psyche. The fight-or-flight instinct has been ingrained in the horse since the beginning of his evolution, and trying to eliminate this instinct brings only frustration and heartache. Instead, focus on building trust and respect with your horse. This will allow him to rely on someone else, namely you, to make some of these decisions for him, eliminating the feeling that if he doesn't look out for himself, no one else will. While you can't eliminate his instincts, you *can* get him to trust you enough to overrule them from time to time.

The instinct to get rid of whatever is on his back is another part of your horse's makeup. Mountain lions and other large cats were known enemies of the horse, and one of the cats' favorite methods of attack was from above. The horse consequently developed a visceral ability to get rid of any attacker that struck from above. Keeping this in mind, it is possible to train your horse to willingly accept objects on his back, including humans, without fear or panic. But it takes time. A young horse will buck, not to be destructive or vindictive, but out of instinct and fear. These issues *must* be addressed and satisfied before any training can take place.

Horses, like humans, have moods. It is impossible for your horse to be "up" all the time. There will be days when he is tired, doesn't feel well, or is just plain lazy. If you own a mare, you may notice changes that correspond with her heat cycles. While most geldings are fairly even tempered, you may have to deal with a little more from a mare. A mare can be moody, and you may need to adapt your training schedule to work around these temporary tiffs. A mare also may be more sensitive to changes in your moods and may react more to energy that is present around her.

When introducing new objects or concepts to your horse, keep in mind the perceptions and instincts mentioned previously. Taking a moment to stop and evaluate how your horse is seeing something may help you introduce your idea in a more appropriate way and may increase your chance of having the horse accept the concept or object. Whenever possible, allow your horse to initiate the initial interest in an object. His curiosity will prompt him to learn more about it and will give you a natural entré for training.

Horse Psychology 101

Although you may be starting with a horse that is seven or eight years old, you must remember that if the horse has had little handling, or only ground basics, your horse is still very young mentally. Much of the information in this chapter refers to a "young" horse. This can mean young physically or young mentally. An older horse that is mentally immature is really thinking at first grade level—you have a big baby on your hands. Be patient.

Training a young horse requires a totally different program than the one you may have used for other horses in the past. A young horse has a different psyche than an older, more mature horse. He can be vulnerable and shy, headstrong and hot tempered, or all of the above. A young horse is just beginning to establish his place in his environment. He is curious about his surroundings, yet a little afraid of almost everything. As he reaches the age of two, he begins to test his surroundings as well as people who are involved in his training. He begins to see just where his limits and boundaries lie and tests how he can stretch those limits to accommodate his own desires. Simple training may turn into a battle of wills, and your once sweet, quiet baby may evolve into a little monster. Don't despair. In most cases, this change in personality is only temporary.

Your young horse must go through this changing and testing to establish his sense of identity, personality, and expression of will. How you handle these tests can have a profound effect on the personality that your horse will have as an adult. If you have a young horse, you probably have seen signs of this behavior. If you are deciding on a horse to purchase, keep this in mind and know that buying a young horse is *not* usually easier than purchasing a more mature animal. While you have the benefit of training the youngster from the ground up, you also have to deal with his growing dilemmas, temper tantrums, and apparent brain failure. All of this can be frustrating unless you are accustomed to dealing with this level of maturity.

You, as the trainer of a young horse, will be tested at every turn. He may try to rear, strike, bite, paw, kick, and attempt many other unpleasant antics. He may suddenly become headstrong and difficult to lead or lunge. The approach that you must take is to be firm but understanding. Your horse needs to know that the rules haven't changed. He still cannot get away with these types of behavior, regardless of his identity crisis. It is important that you, as the handler, remember *not to lose your temper.* He is not acting this way out of spite or malice—he is only testing his boundaries and establishing his personality in the way that youngsters of all types are known to do.

Babies will be babies and young horses are always unpredictable. Just because your young horse has tied easily for several months doesn't mean that someting won't set him off, causing him to fight the tie. Don't worry. This is a natural part of your horse's maturing process. It is best to let him fight it out, decide that the post really won't give, and accept that his battle is futile. Then and only then will he decide that pulling just isn't worth the effort and that standing tied isn't so bad.

Baby or Bully?

It becomes doubly important now to watch for mood and temperament signs with your young horse. Always be alert for a darkening of his eye, or excessive laying back of the ears to determine if this is only baby behavior or if you have a young bully on your hands. A baby will do these things usually without warning and may catch even himself by surprise. A bully, however, is likely to telegraph his intentions and will make it quite clear that he knows exactly what he is trying to do, and worse, that he has no remorse for doing it. A bully needs to be reprimanded more firmly, and you need to be on constant guard until this phase has passed. When your horse misbehaves, reprimand him strongly and quickly by either a tug on the lead or a slap on the shoulder, then immediately ask him to do whatever task you were performing before the misbehavior occurred. If he misbehaves again, reprimand him again, but more firmly. Continue the process until he can perform the task without exerting his own will into the lesson. It is important that you not allow any infraction to slide, no matter how minute. It must become very clear in a short time that it will be more difficult on him if he acts up than if he behaves and does what you ask. Give your horse the benefit of the doubt, but if he proves himself to be a bully, take the upper hand and stop this behavior early.

When working through these difficult times with a bully, get as much information as you can about his background and previous handling to determine if the problem existed earlier, or if the problem developed recently. Find out about any problems that he had in the past and how these problems were handled. If you don't seem to be getting anywhere with your current training methods, you may want to try a different approach. If abuse occurred in the past, keep this in mind and act accordingly. The information may not help you solve the immediate problem, but it will give you empathy and understanding as to why your horse is acting this way and will help you determine the appropriate approach to take during training.

A young horse, particularly a male, can exhibit bully behavior as a way of initiating and establishing herd instincts and male dominance. He may become sensitive around his head and chest (areas considered central to his "space"), and he may become aggressive if you touch him in these areas. Do not allow this behavior to go unpunished, even if the behavior occurs in his corral or stall. Your young male horse must learn that, regardless of his instincts and urges, he must obey your rules and allow you to touch him without responding aggressively. If he is uncomfortable with this, make an effort to touch his head and chest at every encounter. Only by repetition will your colt become used to this handling and learn to accept it as nonthreatening and inevitable.

Crowding and head tossing must also be removed from your horse's repertoire. Again, he is trying to exert control and dominance by using instinctual methods of the herd. These behaviors, while understandable at a young age, should nonetheless be stopped. If necessary, and if you have the skill to use it properly, handle your horse with a stud chain to control his head more effectively until you are sure that this behavior has ceased. Never put yourself in danger, and never allow yourself to be pinned between your horse's body and the wall or rail. This kind of crowding can lead to serious injury, even if he has no intention of hurting you. The goal is to reprimand to correct, but not expand, the problem. Underreacting will not solve your problem, and overreacting will produce a resentful horse. Keep your reprimand in line with your horse's behavior.

Protective Habits

Your horse has many instincts that evolved to protect him in natural situations. Domestication of the horse did not remove these instincts, yet it is possible, through proper training, to override these behaviors and to develop more acceptable responses in your horse. During years one to four, your young horse will develop behaviors and reactions based on his instinctual drives. The way in which you handle and train him will determine whether those behaviors will continue or whether they will be tempered.

Biting is perhaps the most common vice that occurs during these impressionable years. Most of the time, biting is brought about by hand-feeding and inconsistent reprimanding. The hand-fed horse is like a child with a cookie—one treat is never enough. If you give him too many treats, or if you give him treats regularly, your young horse will become demanding and will begin to expect his reward. He will then grab at whatever looks like a hand with a treat. When he doesn't receive a treat, he becomes frustrated and angry. This cycle can easily lead to biting. If you reach this point, give him treats only through his feeder. If you catch this behavior early, your horse will begin to understand that his treats are given randomly and that he has no reason to demand that they be given at all. Once your horse understands this, you can give him treats by hand from time to time and the problem should not recur. If your horse is older and the habit is already firmly developed, you may have to limit yourself to giving him treats only in the feeder.

If you have been inconsistent in your reprimands, and your horse has gone through his yearling and two-year-old years and been allowed to nip or bite, he may now have a serious biting problem. He may nip as a game or as a sign of boredom. If left untrained and unsupervised, he may hurt you or someone else. The only solution is to stop the behavior early or, if the behavior has already developed, to take steps now to correct it. Regardless of what or whom he is biting or nibbling on, stop him immediately and reprimand him consistently. If you need to use a stud chain as a reprimand, use it firmly, giving a quick jerk and then releasing. Continue to reprimand him physically, accompanied by the command "no," until your voice is sufficient to stop the behavior. A horse of this age will usually nibble or test whatever he is thinking about nipping. The first few times you may think that this is cute, but remember that it is a prelude to biting. Stop this behavior now and save some headaches later.

Kicking, striking, and rearing all evolved as defensive behavior, play techniques, and demonstrations of aggression. In a horse's natural setting, this behavior determines the pecking order and any change of command within the herd. In a domestic setting, however, these activities can be dangerous to the handler and to other animals. Any of these behaviors should be punished unequivocally. If your horse exhibits any hint of these habits, correct him immediately and punish him enough so that he will think twice before attempting it again. If he falls into this pattern frequently, you will need to watch him constantly until corrective training is complete. Even then, be careful that you are not caught off guard in case a relapse occurs. Striking and rearing occur most often in young male horses, especially when around other male horses. Be cautious if you are leading near a stallion or an aggressive gelding. Their presence may cause your otherwise quiet colt to become aggressive and may prompt an attempt to strike or rear. If the behavior starts to happen frequently, use a stud chain to lead your colt, and reprimand him consistently until the problem has passed. Be sure that the stud chain is over the nose rather than under the chin. This configuration will give you adequate control while discouraging rearing. Be careful, however, not to reprimand him too harshly. For your own safety, make sure that you lead your horse at your shoulder, never behind you, so that you can avoid flying feet if he does rear. This also allows you to keep an eye on your horse at all times. Staying vigilant will help to keep you safe. If the problem continues, get a trainer to help you.

Bucking is one of the most visceral reactions possessed by a horse, and it may be your horse's defense of choice. Whether he is scared, angry, or frustrated, he just wants whatever is bothering him off of his back. Bucking is his way to accomplish it. If you stop this behavior early, you will be able to train your horse to express his frustration or anger in other ways. It is a matter of making it tougher on your horse if he bucks than if he behaves. By turning him in tight circles and using the crop in a regulated manner, you should be able to stop the bucking in a fairly short time. If the condition becomes chronic and you feel that you are at risk, get some help in working through the problem.

Spooking is perhaps the easiest instinctual response to curb if it is caught early. Spooking occurs when a horse perceives movement or shading to be a threat to his own well-being. A young horse is more likely to spook at even innocuous objects because of his heightened sense of what could be threatening and a lack of confidence in himself. Not only is he extremely sensitive to his surroundings, he is afraid of almost everything, and his natural response is to bolt. Your young horse needs to be exposed constantly to normal but scary things and be taught that those big, flappy objects are a part of his environment and will not hurt him. Always allow your young horse to look at and approach anything that he perceives as a threat. Have him approach slowly, but make sure that he continues to move forward until his nose is touching whatever he is afraid of. Do not allow him to run away, and if he tries, make him go back to the object. More important, never reprimand your horse for reacting out of fear. This will only exacerbate the problem and teach your horse that he has more to be afraid of than he originally thought. Instead, encourage him forward and let him know that you have confidence in his abilities. Continue working with him until he can approach the object with a minimum of snorting and blowing and until he can stand quietly next to the object. Be firm, but understand that his fears are legitimate.

When faced with these problems, consider their source and act accordingly. Try to understand why your horse is behaving the way he is, and you may be able to determine a creative way of solving the problem. If not, take it slowly and give your horse confidence while maintaining the ground rules. Regardless of how angry you get, overreprimanding your horse will not solve the problem. Don't be afraid or even hesitant, however, to take a firm stand and stick by it. A word of caution: If you feel yourself getting angry, don't take it out on the horse. You will do more harm than good, and it may set you back several weeks in your training.

Instinct Versus Command

As you continue training your young horse, or any horse that has been handled very little, remember that you are working with an instinctual animal. You will often ask your horse to go against his very nature and to quell his instincts in order to perform in the manner that you expect. Some horses trust easily and have no problem overcoming their instincts. Others may have a more difficult time with this concept and may require additional training to overcome their fears and reactions.

Pay attention to your horse's signals and moods. Is he a morning or an afternoon performer? Is he best immediately after feeding? Do certain situations set him off while others are of no consequence? Later, your horse will be able to work regardless of such minor inconveniences, but at this point in training, little things *do* matter. It may be to your benefit to keep these in mind while working on early training and to work your horse out of these routines at a later stage. Try to make your horse's basic training as easy on him as possible. You will find that by eliminating small, annoying problems, your work sessions will become more lucrative.

Your horse may also have a preference for one side or the other. Always work your horse in both directions to ensure balance, but if he is more comfortable on one side, work him on his off side more often. You may have to do more bending and suppling to that side to get him to perform properly. If you are having a problem with leads, make him lope to the off side until he is as comfortable with that lead as he is with the other. All horses have natural tendencies. By understanding this and considering it while training, you can adjust your methods to make them more efficient and effective.

Watch for fear in your horse's eyes and behavior. A certain task may be especially frightening to him. He may possess a particularly strong instinctual pull of which you are unaware. Try to notice subtle signs in your horse's actions that will alert you to problems. A scared horse can be a dangerous horse, and this can minimize, if not prohibit, the effects of any training. Never force a scared horse into any action. Instead, take a step back and try to see the situation through his eyes. What is the cause of the fear? Could previous handling have caused the reaction? Is something visually disturbing about what you are asking your horse to do? Evaluate the answers to these questions before going forward.

The next step is to reintroduce your horse to the activity while either minimizing the fear factor or allowing him to approach or move forward at his own pace. Going slowly is the only way to handle this type of situation. You must allow your horse to process the information and build trust in your decisions. Allow him to explore the situation or concept and to understand it within his own mind before you proceed. If the fear is visual, let your horse sniff and approach before you attempt to move the object or otherwise make it scarier. Once you sense that he is beyond panic, gently move the object and watch your horse's response. If he starts to bolt, walk him back up and start again. Gradually, your horse will come to accept the fact that this foreign object is of no concern to him, and he will relax.

Whether the threat is real or perceived, it is real *in your horse's mind.* Do not get angry or try to rationalize with your horse, because it will do absolutely no good. You must simply accept that whatever is scaring your horse is real to him and focus your efforts on helping him to overcome that fear. Only by being exposed to a multitude of objects and situations will your horse be able to evaluate what is a real threat and what is not. The more you get him out and around other horses and new activities, the more he will learn to accept his surroundings calmly and rationally. He must learn to trust you and know that you will not ask him to do anything that will harm him.

When exposing your horse to new situations, rely on your ability to calm him by touch as well as on your ability to use your voice to soothe. Putting a hand on your horse's neck, shoulder, or wither when he is afraid will act as a security blanket, especially for a young, timid horse. Like a human, your horse will respond to the soothing effect of your touch and will take comfort in the fact that he is not alone. Talking quietly will also soothe him and keep him from panicking. When riding, place a hand on your horse's withers to give him a cue that he should stop and think things out before reacting. This reminds your horse that you are there and that you will help him make the decision to stay or to flee.

Only through patience and trust will you be able to overcome the strong instincts that are present in all horses. By understanding that these instincts exist, you can gear your training toward trust and acceptance rather than toward fear and coercion. Your horse can be bullied into some semblance of behavior, but the moment something goes wrong, he will revert to his own proven instincts and will leave you to fend for yourself. By taking the time to build a bond with your horse, you will create a trusting partnership that will provide the foundation for successful training.

When you take these lessons slowly, case by case, you will be able to override your horse's natural instincts, and he will learn to trust you enough to allow you to make the decisions. These learning sessions will prove invaluable as you progress to training under saddle or over scary objects such as black plastic or water. They will also serve you well in panic situations where your horse can be seriously injured if he does not listen to you. Even lessons such as tying and bathing will be easier if you gain this trust and respect early in your relationship.

Temper, Temper

Although all horses process information in a similar manner, not all horses are created equally. Some breeds tend to be more hotheaded or volatile than others. While exceptions certainly apply, these tendencies pop up frequently enough to be mentioned. Specifically, hotter breeds include Morgans, Arabians, Saddlebreds, Thoroughbreds, and any combination of these breeds. Some of these horses also tend to be highly intelligent—sometimes too intelligent for their own good.

When you are working with a hotter horse, stay on your toes and develop creative training methods to keep his attention. This type of horse does not respond well to extreme force or excessive repetition, and if you use these methods, you will create a resentful, sour horse. Rather than focusing his attention on learning, he will use his mental resources for self-preservation and avoidance. This type of horse can be quite crafty when he sets his mind to it.

If you choose to work with a horse like this, however, you will find that, if handled properly, he is bright, eager to please, and quick to learn. He often possesses a complex, full personality, and, if trained properly, his loyalty is unrivaled. Patience is a necessity with this horse, and he becomes bored quickly. It is a constant challenge to keep training interesting and fun for him. If you can manage this, his training will progress at a lightning speed. As a flip side, he can anger quickly, and if he is in the wrong mood, he has little patience for inconsistency. It is important to keep the ground rules very clear with this type of horse and to stay alert to intentional tests of will. He needs to be reprimanded quickly, then moved on to something else. He will know the amount of reprimand coming to him and will tolerate it if he knows that he was wrong. If, however, you take his punishment beyond the misbehavior, he will become resentful and will do everything in his power to make your life miserable. Keep this in mind before you lose your temper.

Like humans, horses have moods that change from day to day. Mares tend to be more moody than their male counterparts, but all will have occasional days of the "grumpies." Accept this as you would accept a bad day with a friend or spouse. It happens, and nothing in your power will change it. Do not, however, *not* train your horse just because he is a grump. He, like all of us, must learn to control his temper and deal with day-to-day activities regardless of his mood. He may not perform with his usual spark, but he still must perform and do so consistently. Try to be a little more patient on these days and understand that he is doing his best and isn't really up to this. Ask what you normally would, but don't push for absolute perfection. If he performs adequately, leave him alone.

When working with any horse, watch for signs that differentiate between temper and frustration. Unlike humans, a horse cannot tell you when he is confused or frustrated. He may be misbehaving but may not be doing so intentionally. He may just not understand what is being asked of him and may be totally baffled. Out of frustration, he may stop completely or go through "brain fade," where he becomes unresponsive to even the most basic commands.

It is important to recognize the difference between anger and frustration. While the two might occur in conjunction with each other, they should be handled in different ways. If your horse is in training and he suddenly becomes totally unresponsive, stop training for a moment. The confusion and frustration need to be removed, and your horse must be taken back into commands and situations where he is comfortable. Go back to the point where he can perform the task almost without thinking, then try to progress to where you were. If he locks up again, you may need to try a different approach. Horses don't all learn the same lessons in the same way. They have different personalities and perceptions. If one way doesn't work, get creative. Think for a moment of how you would teach another person to do the task, then figure out different approaches to accomplish the same thing.

Once your horse responds to the command and has performed for a few minutes, stop the session. He needs to be praised and have his self-esteem restored. You will gain nothing more by attempting a new activity at this point, and chances are you will be in no mood to try. Always end on a positive note and let your horse know that you appreciate the amount of effort it took for him to overcome the obstacle. Even if it seemed trivial to you, if the obstacle locked him up to that extent, it wasn't trivial to him. Put him away feeling good and let him ponder what he has learned. You may be surprised to know that most of the time your horse will come out of the stall the next day having worked through the lesson and be ready to do it correctly.

It is not a good idea for beginning riders and handlers to work with young or inexperienced horses. A horse needs to be trained with clear and concise direction, which a beginning handler cannot give him. Beginning riders do not have enough confidence in themselves, in their own abilities, or in their knowledge of horses to be firm and clear with a youngster. Neither will they have a clear enough concept of the capabilities of a young horse or how he thinks and learns. How can they expect to give the horse a clear road map when they themselves do not know where they are going? Nor can they judge when they have accomplished enough for one session if they have no idea what a normal training session consists of. You begin to see the dilemma. Only after extensive training or years of hands-on experience and learning should someone attempt to train a young or inexperienced horse without additional assistance. It is best for both the horse and the owner.

Consistency, Consistency, Consistency

When you are training a green horse, especially a young green horse, consistency is of prime importance. A horse at this stage is going through changes daily, and his only hope at gaining stability rests with you. Now is the time to consistently enforce the ground rules that you have previously set for your horse. It may become tiring to watch constantly for misbehavior, to handle your horse's little tests of will, and to stay patient while he tries to drive you up a wall, but your persistence is necessary to maintain consistency. Have heart that this stage will come to an end and that all of your efforts will be rewarded. You cannot afford to let minor problems go unnoticed or you will end up with even larger problems on your hands.

It may not seem like it now, but trust and understanding are being built, even during these trying times. You are helping your green horse to understand that "no" really means "no" and that the rules do not change on a daily basis. Your horse will begin to understand what is expected of him and how he is supposed to behave. Even through your firmness, your horse is learning that you will always be there and that you will not come at him when he least expects it. There are no hidden punishments, and no grudges are held. If he breaks the rules, he can expect a punishment. If he does something right or tries extra hard, he will know that praise or a reward will follow. There should be no guesswork, no mixed messages, and no loss of temper. Keep reprimands consistent and in line with the infraction. Now is *not* the time to teach your horse "a lesson." It will come back to haunt you in the end.

Horses that are young or inexperienced should be handled regularly and, if possible, daily. Boredom and lack of attention will work against you. Your green horse has a short attention span and, at times, a selective memory. The longer he goes between training sessions, the greater excuse he has to claim loss of memory. This can be frustrating to both of you. Consistency is as important in training as it is in reprimanding and praising. Your horse needs to be schooled over and over with the lessons that you are trying to teach. At first, your lessons should last no more than one-half hour. If done on a consistent basis, these lessons will become second nature to your horse. If not, you will have to retrain him at the beginning of every session and hope that you can get enough done in the final minutes that the lesson will stick in his mind. If you work inconsistently, you are always trying to play catch up—and your horse knows it. This soon leads to shortened tempers on the part of both you and your horse.

This is an especially tough time for a young horse. It may seem like you are always picking on the youngster. To ease this situation, you may want to allow minor offenses to pass when your horse is in his stall or pen. This does not mean that biting, kicking, rearing, or any other major offense is tolerated. It only means that he can misbehave just a little, and only in his pen. There will be plenty of time later to tighten up his stall manners.

Play is particularly important to the young horse as he works through this transition. Make sure that your training schedule is balanced with lots of free play and turnout. Put a cone or ball in his stall for playing purposes, and when you turn him out, allow him plenty of time to run, buck, and kick up his heels. Young horses have an abundance of energy. If not given a release, they will turn their energies into more destructive behavior. By allowing them time to themselves in a large area to play, much of this energy will be tempered, and learning can occur.

Sensory Training for Saddling

As you train your horse, it is important to work equally on both sides. This holds true for touching and handling as well. If you are working with a young horse that has not yet been broke and is small enough to still be manageable, you are at a bit of an advantage. You will be able to use a technique called sensory training, a process of desensitizing your horse to various types of handling. The leg technique described earlier is part of sensory training, and various techniques will be presented throughout the book.

To prepare your young horse for saddling later, lean across his back and wrap your arms around his barrel, approximately where the girth will go. If you can grasp your hands, do so now. If you can't, do the best that you can. You want to put rhythmic pressure around the foal's barrel in a pulsating motion. Squeeze your arms as hard as you can, then release. Have someone hold your foal's head and keep him quiet while you work. Don't forget to talk to your foal to reassure him that you are not going to hurt him and that there is no reason to get upset. Do this for five to ten minutes every day until your foal relaxes and accepts the pressure, then reduce the repetition to once or twice a month to remind your young horse of the lesson.

If your horse is too large to practice this training but has not yet been put under saddle, there are other things that you can do to make this transition more successful. With the flat of your hand, put pressure on your horse's sides, estimating where the girth will go. Press in for several seconds, then release. Move your hand up a few inches and repeat the procedure. This will accustom your horse to pressure from your hand and from other external sources. Using a surcingle on a young horse will also accustom him to the pressure that he will encounter when saddled.

In addition to accepting pressure around the girth, your horse must learn to accept the pressure that will be placed on his sides by your legs. This, too, can be taught before you actually saddle your horse. With your hand flat against your horse's side, press in gently until your horse moves away from the pressure. When he does, praise him and try it again. This is the beginning stage of yielding, and it will become increasingly important as your training progresses. This training also familiarizes you with the location of the pressure points on your horse's body. The more you learn about your horse now, the more you will understand his reactions and movements later in training.

Using a surcingle is one of the easiest ways to accustom your horse to the concept of a saddle. A bareback pad also works well for this purpose. Lunge your horse with one or both items before you attempt to put a saddle on his back. Also, introduce him to a bridle and have him learn the basics of giving down to pressure and bending from the bit. To accomplish both of these tasks, use side reins and ground-driving drills. Your horse is not ready to be put under saddle until he can perform confidently and comfortably with these appliances.

At this point, you can also accustom your horse to accepting weight on his back. This can and should be done first from the ground in order to maintain safety for all involved. Lean across your horse's back and gradually allow your weight to rest on him. When he accepts this, get a step stool to put you higher off the ground, then repeat the lesson. Eventually, you should be able to place your entire weight across your horse's back without having him bolt or panic. It is important to have someone hold your horse's head while you work rather than using a tie rack, at least until your horse is comfortable enough to stand without being frightened. While you lean on his back, pet and talk to your horse so that he becomes accustomed to your voice and will accept the movement on his sides. Your young horse frightens easily, and taking your time will benefit both of you.

Training Basics

After the initial bond has been formed, if you feel confident that your horse understands where the boundaries of space are defined and if you have a pretty good idea how your horse perceives life and you, it is time to set some rules. Before you are ready to do that, however, you must understand some basic concepts of handling horses.

You have heard the saying, "Do unto others as you would have them do unto you"? Well, horse trainers could benefit from this philosophy, too. People tend to look for a quick fix in schooling their horses. While this may work for a time, the results rarely last over the long haul. More often than not, the "Ninety-day wonder" methods cause problems in the future.

Training a horse takes time—a lot of time. You will not wake up in the morning and have a perfectly mannered horse any more than you will wake up in the morning and have a perfectly mannered child. It just doesn't work that way. You must learn to relate to your horse. Notice I said relate—not bully, coerce, bribe, or trick—but relate. Approach your horse as the intelligent creation that he is and you will have a longer and happier relationship.

Where To Train

I cannot stress enough that his stall or the corral where he is stabled is *not* the place to train your horse. Don't fall into the trap of training your horse in his corral just because it is handy. If you are serious about training, take him to a fenced, "neutral" area where both of you can get down to business. This lets him know that you are serious and that you expect his attention.

Try to work in reasonably quiet, enclosed areas. This does not mean that your arena needs to turn into a library zone, but loud shouting, screaming, and waving of arms will do nothing to relax your horse and promote learning. Whenever possible, train in an enclosed paddock, round pen, or arena, just in case your horse becomes startled and pulls away. It is easier, not to mention safer, to chase him in an enclosed area than to chase him down the street.

Never forget while working with your horse that you are handling a 500- to 1,300-pound animal significantly larger than you are and therefore difficult to overpower. Avoid training in areas that are too closely confined. Invariably, these situations can lead to your being pinned against a wall or pole, resulting in serious injury. Also avoid areas with low ceilings on which the horse could injure his head. If he has a tendency to rear, or if you will be doing something that could make him throw his head, move outdoors where his chance of injury is minimized. Horses remember these kinds of episodes, making future training more difficult than it needs to be.

Never Frighten Your Horse

A good trainer is especially concientious to never intentionally frighten or startle a horse. Frightening a horse will only teach him that he cannot rely on you for protection and safety. Whenever you work with a young horse or with a horse that is new to you, be aware of your movements. This type of horse is often unsure of himself and wary of his new environment. Any sharp or quick movement could startle him. Practice moving quietly around your horse and you will be amazed to see his anxiety decrease. One sign some horses give to indicate relaxation is lowering the head and licking the lips. You can watch for this when you praise your horse for concentrating and performing correctly during any phase of training.

Reprimanding a horse when he is scared is rarely useful and often leads to increased panic. It can be very tricky, however, to determine when your horse is reacting out of fear and when he is misbehaving. Watching his eyes will give you a strong clue. If he steadfastly refuses to do something, or if his eyes are the size of saucers, you can bet he is reacting out of fear. A horse has an exceptional memory, and training can often trigger the recall of an event that previously terrified him. Be sensitive to this. Give your horse the benefit of the doubt. Stop, take a step back, and proceed slowly and cautiously, and, of course, with lots of praise.

Be Consistent

Just like a child, your horse thrives on consistency. The basic rules must be clear and they should rarely change. This means that you have to be vigilant in enforcing the rules. If you have taught your horse that no nipping is allowed, stick by it. If he happens to get in a playful nip, reprimand him. There is no room in training for ambiguity. Say it, teach it, mean it, and stick by it. "No" means "no" and there is no room for discussion, just as "Whoa" means plant all four feet and don't move. You get the point.

Plan Your Training Sessions

It is important that you train in complete sequences. This means that you have to think a little about what you want to accomplish in a session, then take the appropriate steps to accomplish it. Keep in mind that your horse has a limited attention span. The younger the horse, the shorter the attention span. Do not expect miracles. Do not think that a horse can be completely broke under saddle in one session. It is possible, however, for a horse to get the basics of lunging in one lession. Set realistic goals for your training. Keep sessions short. Work until you get at least some success toward your goal.

Another golden rule is to *always end on a positive note.* Even if the entire session is a battle, find something that your horse does right, praise him, and end it there. Your horse remembers more than you realize, and if you leave a bad image in his mind your next lesson will be even tougher. If you end on a positive behavior, both of you will leave the session with a sense of accomplishment.

Tools of the Trainer

The key concept to success in horse training is: *humane but firm discipline is of utmost importance.* Too often trainers go to opposite extremes and either approach produces an upset or spoiled horse. Being firm does not mean to lose control and go after your horse to "teach him a lesson." Neither does "humane" mean to smack your horse gently on the shoulder and say "Bad Boy" after he has come at you with teeth bared. Moderate, consistent discipline is absolutely necessary for successful training, and punishment should be in line with the intensity of the misbehavior. If the infraction is small, a simple "No" might do. If you get the distinct impression that the horse is out to get you, do not let this go. Discipline clearly and succinctly, then go on.

The choice between punishment, reward, or coaxing in training is a judgment call that you will have to make. Different situations call for different motivations, and you may start with one and switch to another. Basically, it comes down to this: If your horse is purposefully misbehaving or is acting in a way that could be dangerous, punishment is called for. If your horse is walking the line between misbehavior and not paying attention, a reprimand (not quite the severity of a punishment) is called for. If he is being asked to overcome a fear that developed previously, coaxing and praise are called for. When your horse is being asked to do something for the first time and does it, a reward is called for. Of course, many situations will cross and divide these guidelines.

Your Voice

Horses react well to voice commands, and using your voice can make training much easier. This is true for both ground handling and training under saddle. In order to be effective, voice commands must be used consistently and firmly. One of the most common mistakes of beginning trainers is to give the commands in a quiet or sing-songy voice. Your horse learns quickly what tone of voice you use when you are asking and what tone of voice you use when you are demanding. Always use a strong, deep voice when giving vocal commands and your horse will soon learn that these commands must be respected and obeyed. A harsh "Quit" or "No" will go a long way if used effectively, and it should always be your first reprimand. If the horse continues to misbehave, make the voice more firm. Unless you are in danger, always give your horse a chance to correct himself. Again, consistency is very important. Use the stronger tone of voice only if you are prepared to back it up with a stronger reprimand should this one be ignored.

Reprimands

Reprimanding a horse can be done in a multitude of ways ranging from vocal inflection to the use of a whip. Choosing your reprimands carefully is the easiest way to prevent future problems in training. Take, for example, a horse that bites. Your first instinct is probably to nail him on the nose every time he tries it. Let's examine what this might do.

The first several times that you smack him, he probably will be taken off guard and the reprimand may have some effect. Your horse will soon learn your reaction, however, and will start to avoid it. The next time he nips and you swing at him he will lift his nose out of range. Now you have started a game. He bites, you swing, he avoids, and he gets the last word—not a productive scenario.

Now let's say that you take a different approach. The next time your horse tries to bite, you flat-hand him on the shoulder hard enough to sting. It is very difficult for him to get his entire front end out of the way, which means that he may think twice before checking your fat ratio again.

Learn to think ahead and evaluate what future reactions your current correction will cause. Play a game of "what if" with yourself and you will be amazed at the possibilities. It makes sense to choose your reprimands carefully.

Start with your voice and try your horse again. If he continues to misbehave, give him a slap on the neck. If the behavior persists, you may need to use a crop or spur. Always gear your reprimands and punishments to the behavior that is occurring, and only increase the punishment if the behavior continues or worsens. Holding a grudge solves nothing, and prolonging punishment allows your horse to forget why he is being punished and therefore confuses him. Get it done, get it over with, and move on.

Punishments

When is enough enough? If, after all of your coercing and reprimanding, your horse is still purposefully ignoring you, it is time to get serious. Using a whip regularly on a horse is not a good idea, but there are times when a whip is not only warranted, but needed. In these situations, do not be afraid to get a little tough (but don't let this be an outlet for your anger). Two hard smacks usually work. Ask your horse again to perform the required task. If he refuses again, repeat the process. There may be a stand-off, but if you are persistent, you will win. Whatever you do, if you start something, finish it. If you don't, you will have double the battle the next time. If your horse will do *part* of what you are asking and if a long, drawn-out battle will ensue if you try to force the issue, stop with the part he does right. Remember—always stop on a positive note and praise your horse for the proper behavior, even if it isn't everything you had hoped.

Setting Ground Rules

Every horse from weaning to maturity should be taught some basic ground rules. Acceptable behavior has as many definitions as the dictionary, but there are some guidelines that you can use to define acceptable behavior for your horse. If your horse does something that scares you or makes you uncomfortable, it is unacceptable. If he does something that drives you up the wall and makes you head for a padded room, it is unacceptable. And if your horse does something that could injure you, another person, or another horse, it is unacceptable. Beyond that, the judgment call is yours.

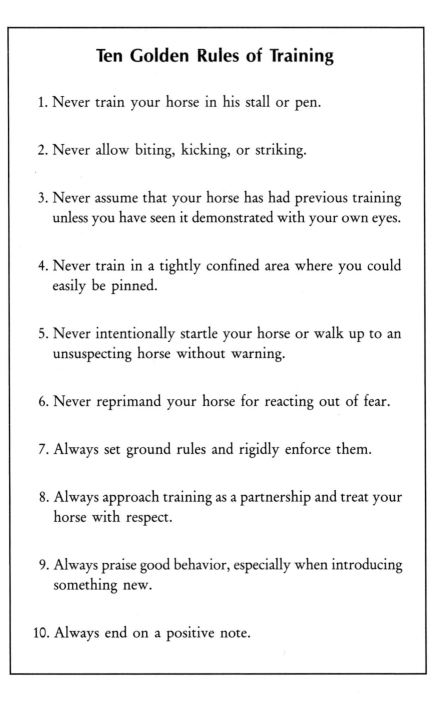

Ten Golden Rules of Training

1. Never train your horse in his stall or pen.

2. Never allow biting, kicking, or striking.

3. Never assume that your horse has had previous training unless you have seen it demonstrated with your own eyes.

4. Never train in a tightly confined area where you could easily be pinned.

5. Never intentionally startle your horse or walk up to an unsuspecting horse without warning.

6. Never reprimand your horse for reacting out of fear.

7. Always set ground rules and rigidly enforce them.

8. Always approach training as a partnership and treat your horse with respect.

9. Always praise good behavior, especially when introducing something new.

10. Always end on a positive note.

The Human Touch

Working around your horse, grooming and caring for him, can be one of the most relaxing and rewarding benefits of owning a horse. Not only do these rituals feel good to your horse, but the physical contact creates a special bond between horse and rider.

When you are comfortable around your horse, you can begin to teach him some basics, such as yielding to pressure. You want him to move away from you as you apply pressure. As you are touching or grooming him, occasionally press against his haunch or shoulder to encourage him to move away from the pressure. When he responds favorably, be sure to praise him. It is not necessary at this stage to reprimand him if he doesn't understand. Continue to attempt the pressure, and be vigilant to catch him doing something right. Positive reinforcement will do wonders to build your horse's confidence and trust in you.

Environment also plays an important part in your horse's handling experience. Horses are not fond of loud noises, sudden movements, and constant activity. Choose a spot to work with your horse that is reasonably quiet and away from the daily hubbub. If tractor work is going on, pick a location a safe distance away from it. If a busy street or road is located nearby, take your horse as far away as possible.

Handling Your Horse's Feet and Legs

Start your young horse on leg handling as soon as he is halter trained. If you have purchased an older horse that has had very little handling, work on this lesson first (after leading and tying). The reason is twofold. First, you need to have your horse's feet workable for the farrier. It is impossible for him to do a decent job of trimming or shoeing if your horse is moving around and refusing to stand or have his feet held. Second, you need to handle the horse's feet when he is tied in order to perform routine hoof care. Both routines are important for sound hooves and healthy feet.

The first step in leg training involves accustoming the horse to having his feet handled. Run your hands gently down the horse's legs and allow your fingers to explore the nooks and crannies of the leg. Next, apply pressure off and on in a rhythmic pulse as you continue down the leg. Your horse needs to get used to someone holding and putting pressure on his leg without him moving or resisting. Do the same procedure on both the front and hind legs. If your horse stomps his foot or tries to kick out, reprimand him by slapping him on the shoulder or stomach and telling him "no." Repeat the process until your horse is comfortable with your touch and until he will allow you to handle his feet and legs without wiggling his body or pulling away.

The horse has various pressure points throughout his body, and the legs are no exception. All of these points are covered extensively in the next chapter, but a few are mentioned here to illustrate how they can be used in routine, day-to-day handling. By familiarizing yourself with these pressure points, you will be able to use them to your advantage in your training.

As you run your hand down the horse's leg, pay attention to the location of the muscles and bones in the leg. Just below the knee in the front, and just below the hock in the back, the leg narrows and becomes sinewy. At the back of the leg, you will feel a hard tendon that

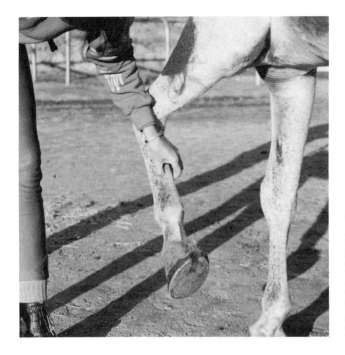

This horse is responding correctly to the leg pressure point. The hoof can now be cleaned or the leg stretched.

runs down the back of the cannon bone and an indentation on each side of the leg. This indentation is a space between the tendon and the bone and is the location of the pressure point that tells the horse to pick up his foot.

To ask your horse to lift his foot, run your hand down to the bottom of the cannon bone, just above the fetlock. Using your thumb and forefinger, put pressure on either side of his leg while saying the command "foot." It may take a few tries to find the right spot, but when you do, your horse will pick up his foot. Be sure to praise him when he responds correctly. Hold his foot for several seconds, then release his leg. Do this training on both front and hind feet, and equally on both sides. As your horse begins to accept this momentary handling, increase the amount of time that you hold his foot off the ground. Eventually, your horse will be able to stand for several minutes while you work on his feet.

Whenever you work with a horse's legs or feet, pay attention to the horse's actions and to what is occurring around him. You may often find yourself bent over and unable to see everything that is going on around you. In these circumstances, you must rely on other senses to detect trouble before it happens. If you feel your horse tense or start to move, look up to see if something is startling him. Do not jeopardize yourself just to make a point.

If your horse begins to panic, release the foot and move away from the horse until you can evaluate the situation. Many times a horse will kick or strike when he perceives a threat. Be sure that you are clear of flying feet should he invent some imaginary danger. Regardless of what is happening around him, your horse should never be allowed to strike or try to kick while you are handling his feet. If he tries, reprimand him immediately with a slap on the shoulder or hip and a firm "No." He must learn that when you are around, kicking and striking are not allowed.

When you hold the rear hoof, keep the foot cocked upward rather than letting it hang straight from the pastern. This changes the leverage on the leg and keeps your horse from kicking with his normal intensity. By supporting the upturned hoof on your legs while working, you minimize your chance of being kicked even more. Nothing, however, replaces using common sense, doing basic training, and staying alert for trouble. Do not allow yourself to be caught off-guard or caught under your horse at the wrong time.

If you are starting a youngster from the ground up, you can give him additional training now that will prepare him for farrier service later in life. If the training is started early enough, trimming and shoeing later will be a breeze. When you handle your baby's foot, use a hoof pick or your hand to gently strike or slap the hoof. This type of "bumping" will prepare him for the cutting and striking that the farrier will do when it comes time to trim. It is easier to handle a startled baby than a startled yearling, and this type of training will decrease his anxiety and make his first trim job a pleasant one.

Desensitization to this procedure will take only a lesson or two, but it will be well worth it when shoeing and trimming time rolls around.

Occasionally, you may have to do stretches with your horse's legs either before heavy exercise or as part of a veterinarian's treatment following injury. This type of stretching is prescribed when a horse ties up or suffers a deep muscle injury, but it can also be useful for the high-performance horse before asking him to reach or jump. Stretches can be done on both front and hind legs. Front stretches stretch the shoulder, the chest, and the upper leg muscles. Rear stretches work the hip, the loin, the gaskin, and the stifle muscles. The stretch that you choose depends on the injury or exertion.

To stretch the front legs, pick up the foot as you would to clean the hoof. Shift your hands so that you have one hand on the fetlock and one just below the knee. Bring the horse's leg back toward the rear until you feel tension in the upper leg. Keep a light but steady tension on the leg for one to two minutes, then return the leg to the normal position, with the foot still off of the ground. Next, put your arm under your horse's knee and lift the knee until it is above the point of the chest in front of your horse. Stretch his knee as high as it will go, and again exert steady tension for a few minutes. In the last stretch, bring your horse's leg straight out in front of him and as high as he can comfortably go without straining. This stretches the back of the leg and the elbow and promotes freer action through the knee and more extension in his reach.

Hind-leg stretches are done in a similar manner. First, pick up the hind leg as you normally would, then bring the leg back behind the horse and slightly upward so that the hock remains slightly above level. Make sure that you maintain some bend in your horse's leg, but raise the leg high enough to lift the top of the hip. You will be able to discern this by watching your horse's croup and seeing if one hip is noticeably higher than the other. Maintain the stretch for a few minutes, keeping the tension constant. Bring the leg back underneath the horse, and, while keeping the foot up, bring the leg under

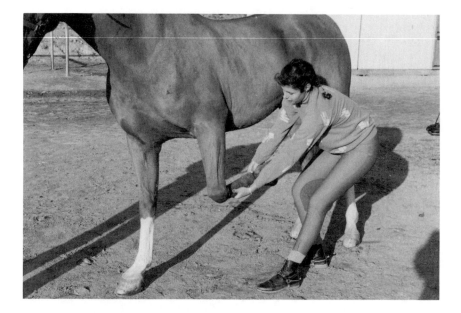

Proper horse and handler positions for front-leg stretches.

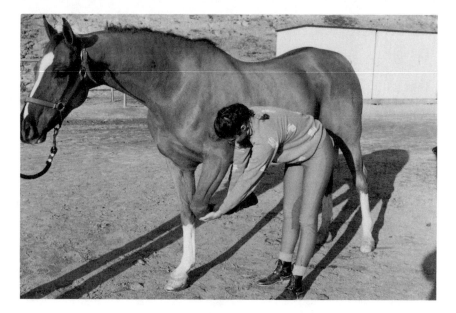

At each position, exert a light, steady pressure on the leg.

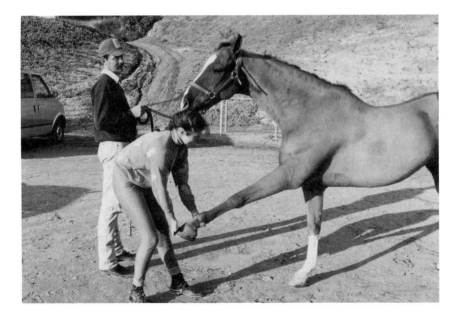

Proper horse and handler positions for hind-leg stretches. Be sure not to stand directly behind the horse and keep the hoof cocked up to inhibit kicking.

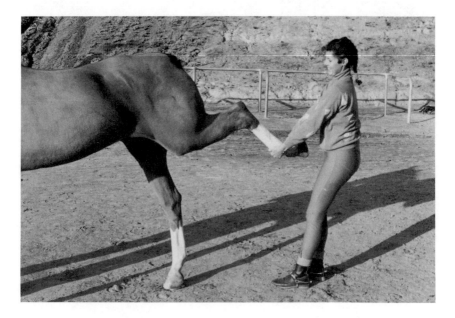

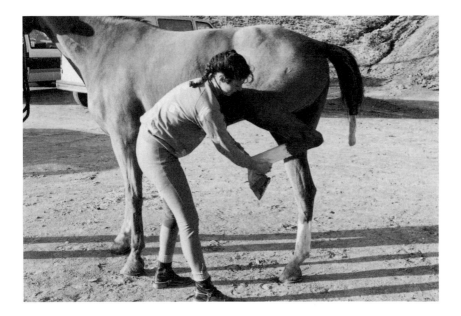

Support the hind leg as you bring it back and be careful to set the foot down gently after the stretch.

your horse's stomach. Hold the leg by the fetlock or pastern and bring his leg as forward and up to the stomach as you can without causing strain. Again, hold for a minute or two, then relax. The entire series will only take a few minutes, but, for some horses, this can cause a dramatic difference in their way of going.

Working Around the Rear

Train your horse to be well mannered when you are working around his rear or giving injections. When you approach your horse from the rear, announce yourself. Before you reach your horse, talk to him and let him know that you are behind him and that you are not some encroaching horse. Remember—he can't see behind himself without turning his head. When you reach your horse, put your hand on his rump to remind him that what is behind him is human and not a threat. Whenever you walk around your horse, stay close to his body and keep your hand on his rump until you reach the other side. If you stay close, your horse will not be able to achieve a full extension with any kick, and this will decrease the effectiveness of any potential blow.

When you handle your horse's tail, stand off to one side rather than directly behind him. It will make you easier to see, and if he does kick, you will be out of the direct line of fire. Your horse may get knots in his tail from time to time, and it may hurt when you attempt to work through them. Be aware of this and be careful when you work on your horse's tail. Keep yanking and tugging to a minimum. If you run across a large knot, work it out with your fingers before going at it with a comb or brush. Your horse doesn't like his hair pulled on any more than you do. Also keep in mind that the underside of his tailbone is extremely sensitive. *Never* use a brush or comb on this soft skin. It will make your horse resentful about having his tail handled.

If you choose to leave your horse's tail unbraided, brush it out regularly to rid it of debris and to remove any knots that have formed.

Wash both his mane and tail at least monthly, and, at the same time, put baby oil or other hair conditioner on his tail and tailbone to prevent itching and rubbing. Also rub conditioner into the skin on the crest of your horse's neck and into the mane itself. Once your horse starts rubbing, it is difficult to get him to stop. This type of irritation can lead to bug infestation or infection. When you wash your horse's mane and tail, rinse all of the soap from both hair and skin. The soap can get caught under the hair and be easy to miss. Watch for this and rinse thoroughly, because the soap will cause severe itching if it is left on the skin. To be thorough, run your hands through the mane and tail several times while running water on it to be sure that all soap has been rinsed away and no residue is left on the skin.

Other rashes can occur if good hygiene is neglected. As your horse works, he builds up sweat between his hind legs and under his armpits. If this is left, it can lead to chafing and skin rashes. To prevent irritation, rinse behind the front legs and between your horse's hind legs regularly, especially after a heavy workout. Run the water between his cheeks, and run your hand between his legs to ensure that no sweat or salt has been left behind. If you have a mare, rinse between the folds of her bag to prevent salt accumulation. Chafing can also occur on the chest and elbow area, so keep on eye on those areas as well.

Good health care dictates that your horse be kept current on several immunizations against dangerous equine viruses. Many of these shots are given in the horse's rump or neck. If you choose to give your horse his shots in the rump, take a few minutes to desensitize him to this treatment. The process is simple. With a closed fist, gently bump your horse on the point of the croup between the bone and the top of the tail where the muscle is large and fleshy. After the bumps, turn the needle, and on the next bump, insert the needle into the horse's muscle. The idea is to get him used to the bumps so that every time he feels them he does not associate them with a shot. Praise him when he stands quietly for you. A treat may also be given to dissociate the bumps from the shot.

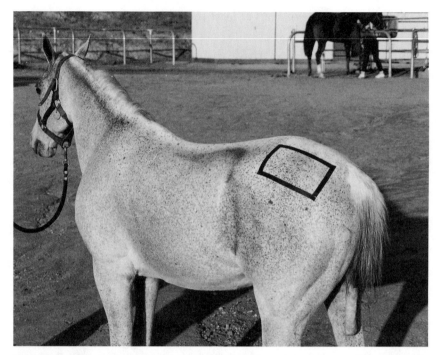

Zone for giving injections in the hind end. Always be sure to stand to the side and stay alert when giving shots.

Desensitizing the Head

Horses are not fond of having their heads handled, but because of the various things that we do with our horses, they must learn to accept handling of their heads, ears, and mouths. If you can start handling your horse while he is young, you will be far ahead of the game by the time you introduce bridles, bits, and clippers. If you have an older horse that is still very fussy about having his head handled, go back to the basics and desensitize him to this type of handling. Remember to move slowly with your training and to never put yourself or your horse in a dangerous position.

The first step in head training is to use the palm of your hand and run it everywhere on your horse's face. Start with his chin and lower lip, then move up to his mouth and nose. Put your fingers under his lips (but stay alert so that he doesn't manage to get your fingers between his teeth) and around the inside of his nose. Move up to his jaw, his forehead, and his eyes. Put your hands over his eyes to actually close them, but talk to him so that he doesn't panic at the loss of sight. Continue up the head to the poll and ears. This is where the procedure may get tricky.

Gently rub the outside of your horse's ears and handle them in your palms. Once your horse accepts this, move your thumb around to the inside of his ear and massage the ear between your thumb and forefinger. As your horse accepts this, gently move down to the inside of his ear. If you ever plan to clip your horse, you will need to accustom him to this kind of handling. You also may need to check for ticks, mites, and other parasites that invade the ear, and your veterinarian may need to treat him to rid him of these pests. If this happens, you will want to be able to handle your horse's ears without starting a war.

Training your horse to accept ear handling may take several sessions, so don't expect him to accept it right away. His ears are one of the most sensitive parts of his body, and he may attempt to avoid your efforts at handling them. Always pay attention to what your horse is doing with his head while you are working with his ears. If you are caught off-guard, you could be injured by his swinging head connecting with your own. Stay alert. Take your time to teach this to your horse, and reinforce the training often.

When you have taught your horse to accept your hand, move on to using a towel. Using the same procedure, run a towel up and over your horse's entire face, including the ears and eyes. At first he may panic, but continue to talk to him and reassure him, and he should quickly accept that soft, floppy object on his head. This training comes in handy when you are applying medication, putting on a hood, or putting a blanket on over his head. If he learns that something is over his head and that he is momentarily blind, yet he is still safe, he will not panic if he ever gets caught in a situation where you have to blindfold him to get him out of danger.

Try to make handling your horse's head as pleasant as possible. If you learn to work in rubbing and massaging motions while handling him, he may even come to enjoy having his head and ears touched. Never move with sharp, quick movements around your horse's head, because you could startle him and cause him to pull back and bolt. Never use anything rough or abrasive on your horse's head. This may lead your horse to resist your efforts, and he may even try to jerk his head away and accidentally injure an eye. Your horse's head, eyes, and ears are as sensitive as yours. You wouldn't want someone running a stiff brush over your eyes or ears.

Bathing

The bath battle has been waged for years. Should you bathe your horse only when absolutely necessary, or should you bathe your horse routinely throughout the year ? How often? This is purely a matter of preference and practicality. If you have worked your horse heavily and there is a film of sweat on his coat, rinse off the sweat to protect his hair quality. But your horse probably does not need a full bath. If, however, your horse gets extremely dirty, or if he is having skin problems, certainly a full bath is called for. Likewise, if you are performing in an exhibition or attending a competition, present yourself and your horse in the most favorable light and give him a complete bath and clip job.

Once you have decided to wash your horse, find a location that is suitable for the job. Ideally, your facility will be equipped with a wash rack and cross ties or a tie rail. The footing should be of textured cement or should have rubber mats with proper drainage. Your horse's head should be secured above the point of the shoulder. If you do not have this kind of setup, choose an open area where you can tie your horse safely and where there is enough drainage to avoid creating a mud puddle.

If you work with a wash rack, you may need to spend some time getting your horse accustomed to the cement, especially when it is wet. Many horses are hesitant to step on this kind of footing because of the illusion that is caused by the darkened cement. To them it looks like a bunch of holes. It will be easier to start with the cement dry, then work up to approaching the rack after it has been used. Make the approach quiet but firm and insistent. With you at his side, lead your horse up to the wash rack and, never hesitating, up onto the cement. If your horse balks, as he probably will at first, stand in front of him and ask him to come forward. As long as he is looking at the rack and is moving or leaning forward, allow him to approach at his own pace. If he begins to plant his feet or to back up, reprimand him sharply with two quick tugs on the lead and the command "no," then immediately ask him to come forward. You may need to enlist the help of a friend who can stand behind the horse and smack him on the rump when he starts to go backward. Continue to coax your horse forward, praising him for each bold step that he takes and consistently reprimanding him if he disobeys.

Now that you are able to get him on the rack, take care not to frighten him. When you introduce water to your horse for the first time, start with his feet and legs. Allow the water to run gently on his legs until he stops snorting and relaxes. Some horses will require only a minute or two to quiet down, while others will require several sessions. It is important to proceed at your horse's pace, not your own, so that you do not cause him to slip or fall and therefore become scared. As your horse accepts the water, progress up to his shoulders and withers. Again, allow your horse to relax before proceeding. Once you reach this point, your horse should allow you to run the water across his back and rump without incident. The problems that you will encounter now will be rinsing between his back legs and washing his face.

When you wash your horse it is important to clean between both front and hind legs and rinse away any residue of sweat and dirt. Standing off to one side and using your hand to clean, gently rub the area as you apply the water. Your hand serves as a washcloth to loosen any dirt that is lodged in the wrinkles and has a calming effect on the horse to keep him standing quietly. Many horses will hunch their backs and scoot their rear ends underneath themselves when they first feel the cold water. Don't overreact and pull the hose away. Instead, talk soothingly and pat your horse on the rump while you continue to apply the water. Within a minute or two, he will relax and allow you to continue.

Start at the top of your horse and work your way down to his legs and socks. When you apply shampoo to your horse, use a stiff bristle brush to work the lather through the coat, paying special attention to the croup area and to any socks or white blankets or patches. The white areas, when clean and wet, will appear uniformly pink and will dry to a glistening white. Use the brush on the legs and body to just behind the ears. After lathering, use your fingers to work through the hair while running clear water on the coat to be sure that all soap residue is removed.

Never use a stiff brush on the horse's face. Not only will you make him head shy, but a stray bristle can cause injury to his mouth and eyes. When you work on his head, turn the water pressure down low and slowly approach your horse's face, starting with the jowls. Run the water gently across the lower portion of his head before proceeding up to his forehead. Allow the water to trickle from his forehead down to his nose and to the sides of his face. Be careful not to get the hose so high that it gets water in your horse's ears. This is very uncomfortable for your horse, and can lead to infection. Apply shampoo sparingly with a damp sponge, rubbing the forehead, the forelock, the bridge of the nose, and the jowls. Using the same technique with a clean sponge, rinse your horse's head completely, ensuring that no soap residue remains.

If your horse is young or absolutely will not yet tolerate a hose on his face, use a sponge and a bucket of soapy water to wash his face. After several times of your squeezing the water out of the sponge and letting it run down his forehead, your horse will allow you to substitute the hose for the sponge. Until then, make sure that, after you apply shampoo, you use plenty of clean water to rinse all residue out of the forelock and off of his face. If you don't, your horse will develop a rash and will rub the hair off of his face.

When your horse has been rinsed thoroughly, use a plastic, metal, or rubber sweat scraper to remove the excess water. If any soap remains in the coat, rinse again. This done, apply a spray-on coat conditioner on the mane, the tail, and the body, avoiding the saddle area (this can cause your saddle to slip) to give your horse that extra shine. If your horse has tall socks, you may want to apply baby powder to them while they are still damp to act as a dirt repellent. When you get to the show or competition, you can brush off the baby powder. It will take the dirt and manure with it and will leave the socks gleaming. If your horse has a long mane and tail, you will want to braid and tie them up now to keep them clean until you reach your destination. You may also want to blanket your horse if he will be standing overnight.

Clipping

When possible, introduce clippers to your horse at a very early age. If you accustom your horse to them as a youngster, you will make your clipping later in life infinitely easier. To introduce your horse to clippers, position yourself in front of your horse and off to one side. While keeping your hand away from your horse, turn the clippers on. Slowly bring the clippers close to your horse's neck area. Gently rub the clippers up and down the horse's neck until he gets accustomed to the sound of the motor combined with the touch of your hand. Once he accepts this, set the clipper body against his neck and allow him to get used to the vibration. When your horse relaxes, move the clippers up to his nose. Again, take plenty of time to accustom your horse to the sound and the vibration that the clippers make.

When you feel that he is comfortable with this, move the clippers slowly up to behind his ears, where the bridle path will be. Do not do any clipping until your horse has shown that he will accept it. It is too easy to cause a nick or injure an eye or ear. Once that kind of injury happens, your horse will associate clipping with pain and your job will become substantially more difficult.

When he accepts the sound behind his ears, move back down to the muzzle and begin clipping his whiskers. Go slowly and allow him to adjust to the different sound that the clippers make while they are cutting. When you are done with the nose and chin, go back up and slowly work on the bridle path. If he is reasonably quiet, you may want to run the body of the clippers on the outside of the ear to see his reaction. Again, do not rush this process. Allow him to adjust in his own time.

If you really think about it, it makes sense that your horse gets nervous when you start putting buzzing, vibrating objects in his ears. One of the horse's main survival senses is his sense of sound. Whenever an insect or foreign object enters a horse's ear, he immediately shakes his head to get rid of it, restoring his proper hearing. Now here comes his owner asking him to ignore this natural sense and to stand quietly while he introduces something that sounds like a large bee. Wouldn't you be a little nervous?

When you ask your horse to accept the clippers, be sure that you have done all of the preliminary steps necessary for your horse to be comfortable with having his ears handled. Desensitization will not occur overnight. Handle your horse's ears inside and out with your fingers, and acclimate him to the point where you can insert your thumb down into the base of the ear without any problems. Once this is accomplished, accustom your horse to the sound and vibration of the clippers before you do any actual clipping. When he stands quietly for this handling, you are ready for the next step.

Before you actually clip your horse's ears, stop and consider if clipping is even necessary. Your horse is naturally equipped with a mechanism to prevent bugs from invading his ears, and this increases his protection against the elements and debris. Why should you remove that? There are only two acceptable answers—for medical treatment or care of the ear, and to prepare for a horse show or event. If you think that a clean ear looks pretty and want your trail horse to look nice, leave his ears alone and allow the hair in the ear to do its job. If you decide to clip your horse's ears, make a concerted effort to keep his ears well protected against flies, ticks, and gnats by using a quality fly spray that you must apply religiously. You must also keep his ears clean of dust, dirt, and debris by wiping them out periodically with witch hazel and a cloth. This will help to prevent irritation and infection of the ear caused by intruding particles. If you have any question concerning the necessity of ear clipping, don't do it. If you must clip, take appropriate steps to ensure your horse's health and safety.

Sheath Cleaning

If you own a stallion or a gelding, you will need to take on the chore of cleaning his sheath. This is not the most pleasant task in the world, but it is important to keep the sheath free of dirt, oil, and smegma that build up with work and use. If a cleaning regime is not maintained, your horse can suffer extreme discomfort and swelling, and the presence of excessive amounts of dirt and smegma can cause serious infection. Either way, your horse will be the one to suffer. Proper sheath care doesn't take that much effort, and with a little practice, you probably won't even have to think about it.

To prepare your horse for having his sheath handled, start with a lot of touching and petting on the stomach. Many horses have ticklish spots, and your horse needs to understand that you are not going to hurt him. When he stands quietly while having his stomach handled, move back onto the sheath. Use clean water (preferably warm), and insert your index finger into the sheath opening. If you like, use a small rag to loosen the smegma and aid in its removal. Be sure that you clean all the way around the opening as well as the entire sheath cavity. You will be removing black flakes that are somewhat greasy and sticky, so make sure that you have removed most of them before calling it quits.

At first, your horse may protest at having his personal parts handled so intimately. If he tries to kick, slap him firmly on the stomach and tell him "no." Start slowly, and spread the cleaning process out over several days in order to acclimate him to this type of handling. Do not use soap, because if you leave some up in the sheath it may cause an irritation or infection. If cleaning is done routinely, plain water is quite effective at removing most of the smegma. The important point is to clean the sheath at least once every two months. When your horse stands quietly for cleaning, the process should take only about five or ten minutes per session. This will aid immensely in preventing infection.

If your horse absolutely will not tolerate your handling, or if you are so uncomfortable with the procedure that you know you will not routinely clean the sheath, have the veterinarian do it professionally. Regardless of the situation, sheath cleaning is an important part of horse care and must not be ignored. With stallions, the importance becomes tenfold. If you are breeding your stallion, you must have him cleaned before every breeding session, and routinely in the off-season. This prevents infection not only to the stallion, but to every mare with which he breeds. Even if your stallion is not used for breeding, teach him early and practice the process religiously. It would be terrible to lose a foal, a breeding sire, or a friend from lack of proper hygiene.

Hoof Care

Hoof care is probably the most neglected of the duties of a horse owner. In far too many cases, a horse is lucky if he is trimmed or shod on a regular basis. Good hoof care is important if you intend to keep your horse sound and functional twelve months out of the year, and if you have an aversion to paying high vet or shoeing bills. The time and money required to care for your horse's feet properly are far less than the extensive time off and care that will be needed later if a foot ailment occurs and needs to be treated.

Preventative hoof care involves only two steps. Every day that your horse is handled, clean his feet with a hoof pick. This implement is available for about sixty cents at any tack store. Clean his foot from the heel to the toe in a downward motion. Also clean the crevices of the frog and check for any rocks or wounds that your horse may have picked up along the way. About once a month (or once every two weeks if you live in a particularly dry area), brush his hooves with a hoof conditioner such as Soundhoof® (Equicare) or Rainmaker® (Farnham) to restore some of the natural moisture that is lost through wear and tear. Do not apply these moisturizers too often, however, because they can lead to overmoisturizing and softening of the hooves, making it difficult to keep shoes on.

If your horse develops thrush, some additional care will be needed. Thrush is a fungal condition that develops in the crevices of the frog of the hoof. It is accompanied by a strong, pungent odor that is clearly apparent when you clean the hoof. The hoof will appear white and chalky when scratched with the hoof pick. You can treat thrush with one of the many available medicines on the market today, including Kopertox® Absorbine Thrush Remedy® Thrush Stop® (SBS), and Equicare's Soundhoof Thrush Remedy® The latter has a gel-like texture and is a nonstaining, clear formula. It seems to penetrate easier than some of the others, plus you won't have to worry if you get it on yourself or your clothes. It is important to get the thrush treated right away and to continue treatment for several days or until the odor disappears completely.

Puncture wounds may also occur in your horse's feet and should be treated right away. A puncture wound can be caused by a sharp rock, a nail, a piece of wire or glass, or any sharp object that your horse may encounter on a trail. To treat a puncture, pour hydrogen peroxide into the wound and allow it to bubble. Do this several times in a row to make sure that the wound is reasonably clean. Then apply an antiseptic to keep the wound clean and to promote healing. If the wound is serious, notify your vet so that you can get your horse on an antibiotic treatment against possible infection. He may also recommend additional treatment. If the wound is treated properly, an abscess can often be avoided.

If your horse does develop an abscess, either from a puncture wound or from a rock bruise, notify your veterinarian to determine proper treatment. Normally, an abscess will be located just under the surface of the hoof or the heel and will feel like a soft, mushy mass. If the abscess is large, your horse will experience discomfort and will exhibit lameness. Even if the abscess is not visually detectable by you, if your horse has been ridden on trails, appears lame, and the unsoundness seems to be coming from the foot area, contact your vet and ask about the possibility of an abscess. It could be deeper than you realize. You may need to soak the abscess with Epsom salts to bring it to the surface, where it can be broken and drained. It will also be important to keep the surface covered and moistened to prevent drying and infection and to allow free drainage.

If your horse's feet seem to be particularly soft or you are noticing a high incidence of hoof trouble, consider putting your horse on one of the many feed-through hoof supplements that strengthen and condition his hooves. The most common is biotin. One ounce of biotin added to your horse's daily feed will dramatically improve the growth and strength of your horse's hoof surface. It can help to prevent quarter cracks, breaking, chipping, and dry hooves and will add to the overall quality of the hoof itself. Biotin cannot, however, assist in thrush or abscesses. These ailments are caused by outside factors and will in no way be influenced by any type of feed-through supplement. If you feel that biotin might be helpful in your particular case, ask your local feed store to give you information on the biotin products that it carries.

You should also determine if your horse needs shoes to protect his feet or if his feet are hard enough that regular trimming is sufficient. Shoeing will protect your horse's feet when they are exposed to rocks, gravel, and hard surfaces. If, however, your horse is older and has never carried shoes, his feet may be tough enough to trail ride without them. To determine if shoeing is necessary, look for cracks and chips in your horse's feet, and examine the occurrence of hoof lameness. If your horse is only worked in an arena a few times a week, shoeing is probably not necessary. If your horse is out on rocky trails or other rough surfaces, shoeing might be wise to prevent hoof damage. In either case, regular trimming is always necessary from the time your horse is a baby to the time he leaves you, and proper hoof care should never be neglected.

It is often difficult to find a competent, reliable shoer, but it is important because proper shoeing can make all the difference in the world to your horse's performance. Don't be afraid to ask others who are involved with horses for recommendations, and always trust your gut instinct when it comes to your choice. The shoer that you choose will have a significant impact on your horse and will be working with you for the entire time that you have your horse. Find someone who is reliable, who returns your calls, and who will explain what he is doing when asked about the horse's feet and their condition. Look at other horses that the farrier has worked on to determine if his work is satisfactory. Make sure that the angle of the hoof is in-line with the slope of the pastern and that the horse has been left with sufficient heel support. Too often a shoer will get into the habit of cutting the heel off and leaving long toes with a long slope to the hoof. This is not proper shoeing and must be avoided. Look instead for a healthy heel (the average is one to two inches) and a hoof that is round and properly sloped.

Once you have found a shoer, have him put you on a regular shoeing schedule. Most horses average between six to eight weeks between shoeings, or five to seven weeks between trims. Explain to your shoer the usage of each horse and if any special shoeing will need to be done. Inform him of any past lameness problems to determine if corrective shoeing or special support might be warranted. If the trails you ride are particularly rocky, or if your horse is exposed extensively to hard surfaces, you may want to consider using pads to help prevent bruising or concussion. Also be sure that the shoes are brought back far enough under the heels to provide support. Each horse has differently shaped feet, and the shoes must be large enough to provide room for manipulation. If, when the shoer is done, your horse's feet appear to be too small for his size, question the shoer about the size of shoes used and why your horse's hooves look so small. If the shoes are too small and your horse's feet are repeatedly forced into those confined areas, he could end up with cracks and, worse, contracted heels. This condition will lead to months or even years of corrective shoeing to restore the original hoof quality. Never be afraid to ask for an explanation or to get a second opinion on the work being done. It is much easier to be safe than to risk months of hoof rehabilitation.

How to Worm Your Horse

Worming your horse is another routine that, if adhered to, will prevent trouble in the future and further ensure his health. Worming will rid your horse of parasites that currently inhabit his body, and regular worming will protect against hatching larvae and reinfestation, avoiding permanent damage to the stomach or intestines. The exterior benefits from worming are obvious as well: better coat condition, easier weight maintenance, and fewer vet calls.

While many older reference books suggest rotating between several wormers to increase their effectiveness, rotating is not always necessary with today's medical knowledge. Two products effectively cover most known parasites from bots to tapeworms—Ivermectin and

Pyrantel Pamoate. By alternating these two active ingredients every eight weeks, you can be assured that, unless he is frequently exposed to new horses, your horse is fully protected from these parasites. Both wormers are found in a variety of name brands and are accessible at any tack store, mail-order catalogue, or horse-care outlet. If your horse is exposed often, consider worming every six weeks and adding one of the Bendazole wormers to your program.

Most horses that have been on a regular worming schedule have little problem accepting wormer via oral paste. The process is simple. Dial your horse's weight out on the plastic plunger, slip the tip of the syringe into the side of your horse's mouth, and keep inserting until your fingers almost touch your horse's lips. With your free hand over your horse's nose for control, steadily depress the plunger until all of the paste has been administered to the back of his tongue. Carefully withdraw the syringe, moving your hand down to your horse's jaw and keeping his nose toward the sky. Keep his head in this position until you see him swallow.

The poll pressure point used while your horse is being bridled or clipped can also be used when worming. If you attempt to perform these tasks without the horse's cooperation, you are putting yourself in a potentially dangerous position. It is hard enough to control the wormer to get all of the paste out without having to do it with your hands six feet in the air. Any oral medication given to your horse is important, and it doesn't do any good to worm him if he ends up raising his head and getting only a fraction of the dose. Instead of fighting him, place one hand on his head and the other on the wormer. Ask him to come to you. If you have gained his trust and have trained him properly, he should drop his head and make your life easier. Better still, you will rarely end up with a blob of white goo on your head while worming.

Rarely will your horse require a chain or further restraint for worming. The key is to be patient but firm with your horse and to keep his nose down while worming to prevent him from putting his head out of reach. Conversely, keeping his head in the air afterward will prevent waste. Be sure that you worm in a confined area, but not in an area with a low ceiling. You don't want your horse to throw his head and injure himself, further convincing him that worming is not fun. Instead, try to make his experience as pleasurable as possible, perhaps giving him a bran mash when it is all over. Aside from the treat aspect, it is a good way to be sure that the wormer has indeed been swallowed.

Administering your horse his wormer by means of an oral paste is certainly the most cost-efficient method. If, however, you suspect that a new horse has extreme worm infestation or damage, contact your veterinarian and have your horse tube wormed. This will give your horse the maximum dosage acceptable and will put the risk of parasite blockage and damage in the hands of a professional. Your vet will also be able to advise you of any other problems that the horse may encounter in the future.

Pressure Points

Side Pressure Points

Your horse has various pressure points throughout his body that can be used to teach him to yield, to give him acupressure treatments, and to relieve muscle spasms and tension. Knowledge of these areas can make your life easier when you are teaching your horse to back, to yield to a leg or whip, to move away from a wall or fence, or to drop his head to accept a bridle. Pressure points are quite easy to use. Once you know where the points are located, you can apply pressure or resistance and train your horse to move away from or yield to the pressure.

When you are grooming your horse, you will often need him to move from side to side so that you can reach all of the necessary places. The pressure point that you use to move a horse sideways is the same point that you use to teach him to yield to your leg. It is located about six inches behind the girth at the center of the barrel. With several straight fingers or your closed fist, push into this area with firm but steady pressure. At first your horse may resist and try to lean into you. Tell your horse "no," reapply the pressure, and tell him "over." When he finally moves away, praise him. It will not take long for your horse to realize that it is easier to move away from the pressure than it is to resist it. Repeat the command for several training sessions until your horse responds correctly and consistently to the pressure.

Once your horse learns this lesson, you can use it to prevent yourself from getting pinned between your horse and a wall, a fence, or a tie rack. As soon as your horse starts to move into you, apply the pressure on his side and tell him to "get over." He should respond quickly, but if he chooses to ignore you, slap him on the stomach and repeat the command. This is often necessary if you are working with a young horse that has his attention firmly focused elsewhere. The point is to act quickly and to be sure that your horse has previously been taught to yield.

Teaching your horse this pressure point allows you to move your horse around on the ground, and it provides you with future benefits under saddle. This particular pressure point is one of the few that is accessible while you are mounted. If your horse already has the concept from the ground, he will learn to respond to the pressure from the leg much more quickly. Simply apply the pressure with your leg instead of using your hand, and ask your horse to move over. After a few attempts, he should get the idea that the commands are similar and should respond accordingly. Under saddle, this pressure point can be used for side-passing, pivots, leg yields, bends, two-track, and moving off and on the rail. You will also use it in a multitude of little ways to position your horse for a given task. Once the basics are firmly ingrained, the rest is easy.

Hip Pressure Points

Similar to side pressure points, hip points make your horse move his hindquarters from side to side. Hip points are a little more difficult to locate, but they are very sensitive to pressure. You usually can teach your horse to yield to them in a quick, easy lesson. These points are located halfway between the hock and the top of the croup. If your

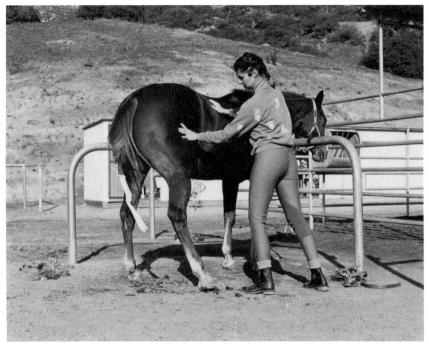

Horse yielding properly to hip pressure point.

horse is in good condition and has good muscle tone, you will see a muscle indentation at the curve of his rump. These points are located in the middle of that indentation. Using your thumb, hand, or closed fist, apply pressure to the hip and tell your horse to "get over." At first you may need to apply a significant amount of pressure to make your horse move. As he learns yielding, less pressure will be needed. Eventually, a light tap and a voice command will be sufficient to make your horse respond.

Hip yielding is also useful for grooming and tacking up your horse. It is helpful for the farrier and the veterinarian in positioning the horse for shoeing or treatment. Use the hip points to get yourself out of the kicking line of fire and to keep from getting caught in a difficult position. Hip points, like all body points, can be used to get your horse off of your foot. If that ever happens, you will definitely see the value of having taught your horse to respond. The use of hip points will also come in handy if you teach your horse to ground drive. Although the contact from the driving reins is slight, a horse that has been properly taught to yield will still move away from the pressure, making it easier for you to keep the horse in line or to enforce a proper bend.

Working with your horse in a confined area can be difficult, and using hip pressure points can make working in a stall a little safer and easier. If you have ever tried to clean a twelve-by-twelve box stall with a yearling that hasn't been handled much, you will understand. While you are working in the stall, the horse may be eating, sleeping, or otherwise not concerned about where you are and what you are doing. To facilitate your task, you may need to ask the horse to move his body or hips to get out of your way. This is accomplished more safely if the horse already knows how to yield. *Never* allow your horse to turn his rump on you in a stall. This makes it too easy for him to decide that this is *his* territory and you are not welcome. If he even starts to turn his back on you, apply pressure to bring him parallel with you or facing you.

Leg Pressure Points

One of the leg pressure points has already been discussed, but another leg point exists as well. Accustom your horse to accepting some leg-pressure cues and moving away from others. Until he learns these basics on the ground, do not put him under saddle.

Your horse has one leg pressure point located about six inches behind the girth. This is your supporting-leg pressure point. Your horse will be asked to accept some pressure on this point and to move away from a stronger pressure. This is different from the other pressure points, but the reason is understandable. When you are riding, you should be able to keep your legs close on your horse's sides for supporting contact and proper equitation. This pressure is a steady, light contact that comes from your legs resting against the horse's sides. When you want to cue your horse, you squeeze with either the right or left leg as a command. This increases the intensity of the contact on the pressure point and changes the meaning of the contact. Your horse needs to be trained to accept light pressure and to bend away from stronger pressure.

The second pressure point on your horse's side is located about three to four inches behind the first. This is your direct-leg pressure point, and it is used as a direct cue for the horse to take a lead or accept a leg yield, or to support the horse's hips and keep them from falling to the inside in a bend. This pressure point is contacted only when a specific cue is being given, because you must consciously bring your leg back from the proper position to use it. Teach your horse to bend consistently away from this pressure, even if the contact is slight.

Training your horse to move away from leg points before you ever get on may seem like overtraining until you have actually done it. Compare the difference between a horse that has been handled this way and a horse that has not and you will find that the trained horse responds more quickly to leg cues and is able to learn circles, bends, serpentines, and correct leads much more quickly. By supporting him throughout his bends and circles, you will help your horse to develop his balance more completely, and he will get less confused when you ask him to collect or extend. It will take him less time to learn to side-pass and pivot, and he will pick up the concept more easily if he has learned these basics. A few days on the ground can save you weeks under saddle. A horse that is older and less side-sensitive will become more responsive and lighter-sided if you practice the lessons from the ground before you ask him to change his ways under saddle.

While working on the ground with many of these pressure points, you may find that your horse has ticklish spots where he is more sensitive to touch, and he may actually pull up and hunch away from you when you find these spots. Ticklish spots usually are found behind the elbows, around the flank, and under the stomach. If you run across a spot that is ticklish to your horse, make a special effort to run your hand across the area frequently to desensitize your horse to your touch before you work on cinching or body clipping. Like a human, your horse needs time to adjust to new situations, and if he knows that no harm will come to him, he will eventually relax and accept the new handling.

Back To Basics

The chest also has one of those useful pressure points, and it is located in the center of the chest where the two major muscles come together in a groove. This point is the key to a successful backing session, and when it is used with other cues, it will teach your horse to back quickly and without resistance. You can apply firm pressure with several straightened fingers or with your closed fist. Apply pressure to the chest and tell your horse to "back." You will need to exert more pressure on this point than you did on the sides or the hips, so keep this in mind when you ask your horse to back. Also remember that, unlike leg yielding, backing is very unnatural for your horse and therefore is more difficult to teach.

Work on backing by using the pressure point until your horse has the basic idea, then switch to using halter pressure as a command to back. For a while, you may need to combine the two to make it clear what you are asking your horse to do. When you ask your horse to yield with the halter, make sure that he drops his head and gives to the halter rather than bracing against it. If he doesn't, work on halter yielding before you teach him to back. To do this, put one hand on the lead and the other across your horse's nose. Apply pressure with the lead, and if your horse brings his head up, apply pressure with your other hand on the top of his nose to bring it back down.

Horse yielding correctly to chest pressure point and light halter pressure. Notice that the horse's concentration is on the handler.

When he brings his nose down, release the nose pressure and ask for the halter yield. Repeat this procedure until your horse consistently flexes at the poll with only the pressure from the halter.

To begin backing, use only halter pressure and your voice to ask your horse to respond. If he ignores you, apply pressure to the point on his chest and repeat the command. At first you may get him to back only one step. This is fine, because he has to start somewhere and should be praised generously for this one step. Continue asking him to back, increasing the amount of steps by one until he understands the entire concept. Praise him after each step along the way to encourage him and to let him know that he is doing what you are asking of him. When he gets the idea with both pressures, switch to using halter pressure only. It shouldn't take long for him to realize that the two cues mean the same thing, and he will respond accordingly.

Eventually you will want your horse to respond to only your voice command and, if you are mounted, to a slight shift in your seat position. Many times when you ask your horse to back, you are trying to manipulate another object *and* control your horse all at the same time. The object may be a mailbox, a gate, or any other obstacle with which you may come in contact. If your hands are busy with the object, you will find it difficult to apply the correct pressure for your horse to back exactly the way that you want. If, however, he responds to your voice alone, you can continue to ask him until he is where you want him to be. Then you can tell him "whoa" to stand still and free your hands to work with whatever object you are manipulating.

To begin this process, start from the ground. This time when you ask your horse to back, use only your voice and say the command "back" without exerting any pressure on the halter. If he does not respond, apply slight pressure to get him started, then immediately release the pressure but continue to tell him to "back." Within a lesson or two, he will begin to anticipate what you are asking and will willingly back when asked. Whenever possible, continue to school him on backing in response to only your voice command to reinforce the lesson. When you start riding, you will be glad that you did.

Head Pressure Points

One of the most useful pressure points for ground handling is located just in front of the horse's poll and between his ears. This point, when used properly, will cause your horse to drop his head significantly, putting his head and ears within easy reach for bridling, clipping, and grooming. The point is found on either side of the point of the poll just above the indentation where the ears are attached.

Like the other points discussed, pressure is used to teach a desired response. In this case, you are asking your horse to drop his head. When you find the points, use your thumb on one side and your

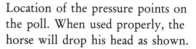

Location of the pressure points on the poll. When used properly, the horse will drop his head as shown.

forefinger on the other, and apply steady downward pressure. If your horse does not respond at first, wiggle your fingers back and forth while applying pressure to get your horse to listen to you. Continue to apply pressure until your horse drops his head. When he does, praise him and let him know that you are pleased. Let your horse stand for a moment, then repeat the command. Your horse should respond more quickly this time. Repeat this lesson several times per training session until he completely understands what you are asking of him. Always reinforce the behavior with sufficient praise when your horse responds correctly.

Bridling

Bridling is one of the most difficult yet necessary tasks that you as a horse owner must master. You won't get very far unless you can bridle your own horse effectively, and he may not always be willing to cooperate. Why does your new horse avoid you and the bridle at

Most
common
method of
bridling.

all costs when you approach him? The answer could be as simple as the way in which you are trying to bridle him.

Your horse is a creature of habit, and he learns by repetition. He likes the routine of knowing exactly what to expect and being handled in the same way time after time. Believe it or not, there are several ways to halter or bridle a horse. If you are doing it one way, and the previous owner did it another way, your horse will resist bridling. If your horse refuses again and again, try another technique and see if you get different results. Chances are, this is your problem.

Two common techniques are used to bridle and halter a horse, and there are probably innumerable variations thereof. The basics are given here, but you can experiment on your own. The first is considered the most standard. Stand on your horse's left side. Hold the top of the bridle with your right hand. With your left hand, let

Most common method of bridling.

the bit rest across your thumb and little finger, with your other three fingers pointing upward. Bring your right hand over your horse's head and center it between his ears, about two inches from his forehead. Use your thumb and little finger of your left hand and slip them into your horse's mouth on either side, putting slight pressure on the bars to encourage him to open his mouth. As he does so, move the bit into his mouth with your left hand, and continue to bring your right hand above his head to eliminate any slack in the bridle. Be careful not to bump his teeth with the bit. Once the bit is in his mouth, use your left hand to help ease the bridle over your horse's right ear and then over his left ear.

The second method is often effective on a younger horse, because it allows you to control his head more easily. Again, stand on the left side of your horse. Place your right arm under your horse's chin

Alternate method of bridling, best used with a young horse to control his head while still maintaining ultimate control of the bit.

and around the right side of his face to the front of his nose. With your right hand, hold the bridle at its middle, keeping both sides of the bridle together below the browband. With bridle in hand, place your right hand high up on top of your horse's nose. Hold the bit as you did in the first method, with your thumb and little finger supporting the bit. Place your fingers in the corners of your horse's mouth and ask him to open it. Slide the bit in and use your right hand to take up the slack, again taking care not to bump his teeth with the bit. Now, use your left hand to hold the bridle while you switch your right hand to the crown. You can now use your left hand to ease the bridle over your horse's right ear and then over his left ear.

Both methods have their advantages and disadvantages. The second is a little more awkward, but it allows you to control the horse's nose and head. This prevents your horse from avoiding the bit. The first

Alternate
method of
bridling.

method is easier to manage, but it offers you no control should your
horse decide to raise his head or turn away from the bit. Both allow
you to slide the bit into the horse's mouth to prevent bumping of
teeth or injuring of gums—an action that can cause your horse to resent
the entire bridling process. Both will take some practice, but feel free
to experiment with them to determine what is most comfortable for
you and your horse.

The bars of your horse's mouth are located just inside the corners
of the mouth. Your horse has no teeth on this section of his jaw,
and this is where the bit should sit comfortably. If the bit is too tight,
it will put pressure on the corners of your horse's mouth, causing
him to gape and chew. If the bit sits too low, your horse will be forced
to try to carry the bit, or he will get his tongue over the top of the
bit, causing you to stop and rebridle him and replace his tongue under

the bit. Adjust the bit so that you can see two small wrinkles in your horse's lips just above the bars of the bit and so that the bit itself sits comfortably on the bars of the mouth.

When adjusted properly, the bit puts very little pressure on the bars of the mouth. Your control comes from the port of the bit or from the break of the snaffle coming into contact with the top of your horse's mouth. This is what tells your horse that you want him to slow down or drop his head. If your reins are relaxed, little or no pressure is exerted. If you take up on your reins, the bit rotates in your horse's mouth and exerts pressure on the roof of his mouth. Some pressure is also exerted on the corners of his mouth, but this is not the primary source of control. If, however, your horse has spurs on his teeth, the pressure on the corners of his mouth could cause the sharp tooth to rub on his cheeks and cause pain.

Your horse's teeth are located in front of and behind the bars of his mouth. Usually, his front teeth require little or no care unless a piece of hay gets caught, causing an infection. As your horse ages, however, spurs often begin to grow on the outside of his back teeth. These spurs can be painful and may interfere with eating and bridling. You can check for spurs on your horse's teeth by running your finger along the outside of his teeth, just above the corners of his mouth. Be careful not to allow your finger to get caught between his teeth or you could get your finger crunched. The tooth surface should feel smooth and free of any sharp edges. If you do feel spurs, call your vet. He will perform a simple procedure called floating, which is actually the rasping of the edges of the teeth to remove spurs. If your horse is suddenly difficult to bridle, or he is not eating as well as usual, check to see if he needs to have his teeth floated.

Tying and Haltering

Much of the information already covered in this book assumes that your horse has been taught to stand quietly while tied. Tying is probably one of the most frequent things that is done with a horse, and therefore it is easily taken for granted. But what happens if you are doing all of the training on the horse or have purchased a horse that has never been taught this necessary skill? Are you doomed to piles of broken lead ropes? Not necessarily. Instead, you will have to teach your horse to tie and to stand quietly at the tie rack while you groom and saddle. What you may not realize is that the first part may be easier than the second. The concept of tying is easy enough to teach, but developing patience may take years to truly ingrain, and even then, memory lapses will most certainly occur.

To start this lesson you need a strong, solid tie rack, preferably one mounted in concrete. The rack itself should be made of thick wood or metal pipe that have had any rough edges removed. Be sure that the wood is in good condition and not rotting or splintering excessively. If you can move the rack back and forth with your hands, it is not solid enough to teach your horse to tie and could cause serious injury. In the absence of a tie rack, use a sturdy tree that has plenty of head room and that is free from debris at the base.

You also will need a strong nylon or leather halter (*not* one of the so-called string halters) and a thick cotton lead rope. Cotton leads are better than nylon leads because they give a little more and will not tighten down on the knot. You also will have less of a chance of suffering rope burn if you need to intervene. The halter should fit snugly but should not bind anywhere on the head. Likewise, the halter should not gape or bag around the ears or muzzle. If it does, get another halter that fits properly.

You should *never*, under any circumstance, tie your horse with a stud chain attached to the lead. The potential injuries, should your horse pull back, are mind boggling, and you will surely create an animal that will be afraid of tying for a very long time. If you are working with a stud chain and need to tie your horse, either remove the chain completely or switch the snap on the lead rope so that it attaches directly to the halter ring.

If your horse has a history of pulling away or breaking lead ropes while tied, you may want to purchase some optional equipment to break this frustrating habit. Several companies make an anti-pull lead rope that flexes and stretches when pressure is exerted. This rope is made with a stretchy nylon, and it can stretch to about four feet in length. When your horse pulls back, the lead rope merely gives with the horse yet maintains tension on the halter. This rope can prevent your horse from panicking because he has hit the end of the rope. It gives just enough to startle your horse into coming forward again. It also teaches him that even if he stretches the lead, he cannot get away. If your horse tends to panic when he feels the pressure of a tight lead, this is your safest bet.

An anti-pull halter will also stop this kind of behavior. It is easy to use and will cure all but the most difficult cases. The concept is simple. A halter is fitted with an additional length of thin rope that is threaded through the ring below the chin, up over the side of the head, around the poll, and down the other side. The rope is then tied along with the regular lead to a sturdy tie rack. Usually these halters are also equipped with a safety release should your horse put himself in danger. They are designed to put pressure on the top of the horse's head as he pulls back and to make it increasingly uncomfortable as he continues to pull. If he stops pulling, the pressure from the cord on his poll is released and he is rewarded. In most cases, it takes only a few lessons for your horse to understand that it is much more pleasant to stand tied than to pull back and cause himself such discomfort.

There are advantages and disadvantages to a leather halter compared to its less expensive nylon counterpart. If used consistently on only your horse, the leather halter will fit more closely to your horse's head and will eventually mold itself to some of the contours that are unique to him and him alone. This close fit will decrease the amount of rubbing and chafing typically caused by a halter. A leather halter also breaks more easily than nylon, which is a good safety feature should your horse get caught in an emergency situation and try to pull free.

On the other hand, because of this added strength, a nylon halter is great for teaching a horse to tie. The lead will probably give before the halter, reducing the amount of money that you have to spend should your horse break away. Nylon halters also last longer and are initially cheaper than leather halters. They are easy to take care of because they can be cleaned with a bucket of soapy water and a stiff brush and hung out to dry. Leather halters must be cleaned with leather soap and conditioned regularly in order for them to retain their elasticity and flexibility (although you must be careful not to over-oil leather because it can lead to rotting).

Always secure your horse with a safety knot rather than wrapping the lead around the tie rack or tying the lead in a square knot. The safety knot is a precaution so that if your horse is spooked or panicked, you can release him quickly and easily without risking your safety or that of your horse. The knot is easy to tie, will greatly increase the safety of your handling, and should be used whenever you tie your horse.

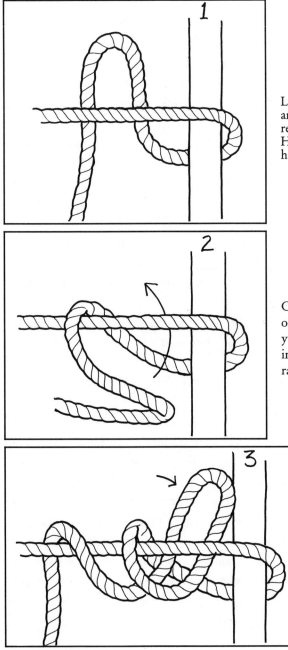

Loop rope around tie rail and form a loop with the remainder of the lead. Hold lead in your left hand.

Cross loop over the part of the rope attached to your horse's halter and insert it between the tie rail and the cross.

Pull the loop snug close to the tie rail.

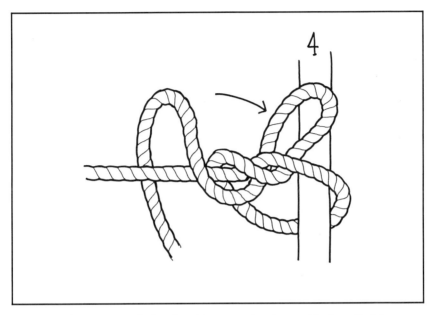

Transfer loop to your right hand and form another loop with the tail of the rope.

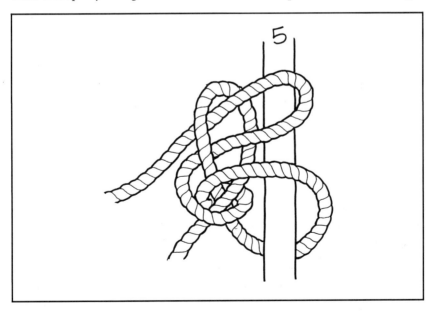

Insert second loop through the loop in your right hand and pull snug.

If you are working with a horse that has never been tied before, take the process one step at a time and allow your horse to understand and become comfortable with each step of the training before you continue to the next step. The first step is to allow your horse to get used to the tie rack itself. Approach the tie rack and let your horse look at it. If he does not spook, bring him up to the place where he will eventually be tied. Ask your horse to stand quietly for several minutes while you hold him, then praise him. Repeat this several times until he stands quietly without fussing.

Next, loop the lead rope once around the tie rail, and, with the end of the lead rope still in hand, again ask your horse to stand. If he pulls back, keep pressure on the lead and pull him back into the rail, simulating the pressure that he will feel if he pulls back while tied. Immediately tell him "whoa." Continue to work until your horse no longer resists when he leans back and feels the pressure of the halter. He must learn that when he does feel pressure, he should go forward rather than backward to relieve the pressure.

You are now ready to try your first tying job. Using the safety knot, *loosely* tie your horse to the rail. The knot needs to be loose enough so that you can easily pull him free if he panics. Stand at your horse's head and tell him to "Whoa." If your horse stands, move away slightly and tell him "Whoa." Gradually increase your distance until you are about ten feet away from your horse.

At this point, your horse will do one of two things. He will either accept the resistance of the tie rack and come into the pressure, or he will decide that he is going to fight. Your first instinct will be to "rescue" your horse as soon as he starts to pull back. Do not give in to this temptation. Move close enough so that you can free him in case he really starts to lose control and tell him "whoa." Keep repeating the command until he settles down, then praise him for thinking about it and making the right decision. If your horse continues to panic and it looks like he will go over backward, or if he thrashes so much that he could injure himself, release him and go back to looping the lead around the rail while you still hold the end. Be very careful to hold onto your horse securely after freeing him. You do not want him to learn that whenever he pulls back, he will break loose. Work on this so that when he starts to feel pressure he will give in to it rather than lean against it. Then try tying again.

After the first "battle," you will probably have minimal trouble with tying your horse.

If you must intervene between your horse and the tie rail, keep in mind that your horse is now reacting blindly without thought for who or what is in his way. Watch out for your own safety. Do not, under any circumstance, put yourself between the rail and your thrashing horse. You will only be asking for trouble. Instead, stay on the opposite side of the rail from your horse and work the safety knot free. You may need to duck under the rail once your horse is released to keep him from pulling away from you, but this is better than becoming trapped by a frantic, one-thousand-pound animal. You are only a fraction of your horse's body weight, and he can easily hurt you in a time of panic. Keep your feet, head, and body out of the way of his thrashing feet or his swinging head, and release your horse only when it is safe to do so. The worst that will happen to your horse is that he will go over backward and bang himself up. You can always cut the lead to free him. If you are not careful, however, you could end up in the hospital with a serious injury.

Never allow yourself to become trapped between a solid, immobile object and your horse. This can lead the horse to panic and can also cause you to become injured. Whenever you tie your horse, make sure that there is room for you to walk all the way around three sides of him and, if he moves into you with his body, make sure that there is room for you to get away. Also check that the footing around the tie rail is free of clutter or debris. It doesn't do any good to have plenty of room if you end up tripping over clutter while trying to avoid a panicked horse.

Young horses that have not been handled extensively can be

especially prone to injury while tied. It is often said that if a baby can find a way to hurt himself, he usually will. Keep an eye on a young horse at all times. Make sure that he is tied securely, yet safely, so that if he pulls back, you will be able to release the lead quickly. Keep large or sudden movements to a minimum, and always talk to your young horse to let him know that everything is all right and that nothing is going to jump out and hurt him. Keep an eye on him, but don't baby him.

It is okay, and even desirable, to let your young horse stand, supervised, for a length of time in order to teach him patience. He needs to learn that just because *he* thinks he is done standing doesn't mean that *you* think he is done. He should stand quietly until you say otherwise. This may mean working him through pawing, pulling back, and pacing. As long as he is not hurting himself, let him work through this. Eventually, he will give up and decide that the effort just isn't worth it.

Don't forget that you must also protect yourself. If you are going to be working with a horse that is known to pull, wear gloves to prevent rope burn. Whenever you work around a horse, wear sturdy footwear to protect your feet in case your horse steps on you. Most important, stay aware of the situations into which you are putting yourself, and avoid any instance where you are likely to become injured. By thinking ahead, you can avoid trouble for both yourself and your horse.

Haltering the Ear Shy Horse

Ear shyness is one of the most common complaints of horse owners. Whether the aversion was caused by frequent earing (using the twisting of an ear to maintain control or to punish) or by a lack of proper early handling, an ear-shy horse will pull his head away, either to the side or up, whenever you try to bridle, clip, or even clean his ears. He will resist any attempt you make to handle his ears and may go so far as to swing his head abruptly into yours. If your horse is indeed ear shy, you must work carefully to correct the problem, always staying alert for the possibility of his head aiming in your direction.

If you have a young horse and have practiced the touch techniques presented in Chapter 4, you will now begin to reap the benefits. Instead of having to hassle with simple tasks such as bridling and haltering, you will be able to skip this section and move on to other lessons. If you haven't taught your horse to respond to pressure or spent the time handling his ears, you will now need to work through these battles in order to continue your horse's training progression.

Trying to halter a horse that is severely ear shy will create problems of its own. You may be able to comfortably get the halter around your horse's nose, but when you try to flip the strap around the poll, your horse will likely pull away and run laps around his pen. If this occurs, you will have to begin your horse's training using only a rope around his neck to form a makeshift halter. Put the lead rope around your horse's neck, with the clip end on the near side. Cross the two loose ends under the horse's throat so that the clip end is now on the off side, and bring that end over the top of his nose and back to your hands. Adjust it so that the slack is removed and clip the snap onto the rest of the lead rope. You will now have a figure-eight halter that will work fairly well to control the horse while in his pen.

Next, run your hand up the horse's neck toward the poll, scratching as you go. The idea is to make this as pleasurable as possible for your horse. Slow down as you get close to his ears, but continue to inch your way along. If your horse tries to raise his head or pull back, tell him "no," but keep your hand in position. Try to avoid removing your hand completely. As you reach the poll, pause and let him get used to your touching him this close to his ears. Play with his forelock,

Figure eight halter made out of a lead rope. This is only used as a temporary means of control while in a pipe corral or closely confined area until the horse can be properly haltered.

scratch the base of his ears, and just move your fingers around. When you feel him begin to relax, work your hand up around the base of his ear and begin rubbing gently, starting with the outside.

If you have had a battle to get to this point, stop here and praise your horse for his tolerance. If things have gone smoothly, continue so that you are rubbing the inside of his ears with your thumb. Again, try to make this as pleasurable as possible. You want him to know that you are not going to hurt him and that having his ears handled really isn't so bad. This is where you may have some trouble. Do this very slowly, and praise your horse profusely along the way. It may take several sessions for you to even get close to touching the inside of his ears, but with patience, you will eventually be able to rub the insides enough to clean and care for his ears. Try not to turn this into a battle of wills. Go slowly and let your horse know that having his ears handled is unavoidable but tolerable.

When your horse allows you to handle his ears, go back to haltering him with a normal halter. Approach him slowly and talk to him constantly while you work with the halter. As you approach his ears, scratch his neck for a moment, then gently flip the strap over his poll. Be sure that the lead rope is also around his neck in case he tries to pull away. It will give you something to grab onto so that you can regain control. Practice this several times until your horse is comfortable being haltered.

Now that you are able to halter your horse easily and handle his ears with a minimum of resistance, take your horse out of his stall and try to bridle him. In Chapter 6, bridling variations and their benefits were discussed. Start with the second bridling technique, and gradually progress so that you are able to move into the first technique. The second technique will give you more control over the horse's head and will allow you to progress more slowly when slipping the bridle over his ears. In time, however, your horse should become tolerant enough to allow you to go directly over the top of his ears and rest the top of the bridle on his poll. Remember that whenever you are working with a horse that is ear shy, stay alert and prevent yourself from getting smacked in the head.

If you notice that your horse is shaking his head excessively or appears to be trying to rid himself of an unwanted pest, stop and check his ears to see if a bug or tick has worked its way into the ear canal. If your horse is tolerant, clean his ears with witch hazel and a soft cloth to remove any excess dirt and oil that has accumulated, then apply fly spray sparingly with your fingers. If the situation persists, call a veterinarian to check more thoroughly for pests or skin problems. While riding out on trail, your horse can pick up ticks that will burrow into the ear and cause extreme discomfort. Rather than battle your horse and possibly injure yourself in the process, allow your veterinarian to professionally clean and check your horse's ears and to rid them of any parasites. Never allow your horse to shake his head for more than an hour or so. If he is this uncomfortable, he could give himself a concussion from a blow against a pen rail or the ground.

Leading and Ground Manners

Again, you should never take for granted that your horse, even a seasoned saddle horse, has been well schooled in all areas, especially ground manners. And even if he has, a little refresher course may be called for occasionally.

A well trained horse will walk quietly at your side, his shoulder even with your shoulder, without crowding or dragging you as his handler. If your horse doesn't behave this way, or if you are working with a young horse, start at the beginning to correct these problems and establish control before you proceed to other areas of training.

"Whoa" Means "Whoa"

The first and most important command that your horse should learn is "Whoa." This is the one command that should be enforced, unfailingly, throughout your horse's life. It is the one command that may save you and your horse from serious injury, and it may prevent many minor catastrophes along the way. For this reason, drill it

This horse is responding to the verbal and pressure command of "whoa."

unmercifully until it is so ingrained in your horse's mind that he wouldn't even think to ignore it.

Your first training of this command will occur on the lead line and will then progress to the lunge line, to the tie rack, and to being under saddle. On the lead, start your horse responding to "whoa" the day that you get him or the first day that you work on leading. Devote at least ten minutes each session to stopping on command until your horse responds consistently and unfailingly every time he is asked. Quite simply, "Whoa" means to stop now, plant all four feet, and don't move. While your horse is on the lead line, walk around him at the end of the lead repeating the command, making sure that he stands quietly. If you are working on this and your horse takes even one step, give him a sharp tug on the lead and repeat the command. You should be able to walk from one side of your horse all the way around to the other side, and from front to back, without him moving even one step. Also work on walking away from your horse after telling him to whoa, and on having him stand rather than follow you. He should not move until given the command to move. If he does, he must be reprimanded.

Once your horse gets the hang of stopping on the lead, progress to training with the lunge line. It shouldn't take him long to figure out that the same rules apply to both leading and lunging. Whenever you are lunging, practice stopping from every gait and in both directions. Your horse should respond within a maximum of two or three steps at any gait. If he does not, reprimand him. When he does perform correctly, praise him and let him know that he is performing correctly. This schooling may seem tedious, but when it prevents injury to yourself or to your horse, you will be glad that you took the time to do it properly.

The tie rack is another place where "whoa" should be enforced rigidly. This applies to your horse pulling back against the rope and moving from side to side while you are grooming or tacking up. If your horse starts to pull or move aside, tell him "Whoa." If he doesn't stop immediately, give him a sharp tug on the lead. You can do this even if the horse is tied. Just use the portion of the lead rope between the tie rack and the halter. If he has been schooled, he will know what it means, and you will not have to pull very hard. The point is to let him know that you still mean it even though he is in a different situation.

By schooling your horse consistently, you will ingrain the concept into his mind so deeply that you will often be able to override his panic in a crisis situation. The first step that you should take if your horse gets tangled in rope or wire or caught in a fence or in mud, or if he finds himself in any dangerous situation, is to immediately get to his head and tell him "whoa" in a voice that demands attention. If you can get close enough to put a hand on him, do so. This will reinforce your presence and shift his attention away from whatever is scaring him. If you have trained him properly, he should freeze.

The quieter your horse lies or stands, the easier it will be to get him untangled or work him out of a difficult situation. It will also allow you to work more safely around your horse's legs. You should still be very careful when working around any panicked horse, yet this simple command will often allow you to freeze the horse's motion enough so that you can physically move his legs and get him out of the predicament. It takes only one time to make you appreciate all of the hard work and drilling that you did earlier in training and to make you a believer in a firm "whoa."

To Back Or Not To Back

When you are teaching your horse to back, remember that a horse does not naturally back up for more than a stride or two. What you are asking him to do, therefore, is rather foreign. To you it may seem like a simple task, but to your horse, it might seem mind boggling. Repetition, patience, and drill are important for success.

The first step in backing is to go back to the basics of yielding to pressure. If you are having problems, you may need to go back and review the section on pressure points, then apply that knowledge to the following information.

As mentioned in the chapter on pressure points, the main pressure point for backing is located on the chest. Use a plain halter without a chain to teach your horse to back. A chain will cause pain, and your horse is apt to resist the training and spend most of his efforts bracing against the chain rather than learning. Gently place your fist in the center of your horse's chest and, with your right hand on the halter, use halter pressure and ask him to back. Also use the command "back." Don't worry right now if he backs straight or not— merely focus on the concept.

At first your horse will be totally confused. This is normal. Keep repeating the command and applying pressure until he yields one step. When he has accomplished this, praise him profusely. He needs to know unequivocally that he has performed correctly. Now try two steps. Again, praise him dramatically and continue to praise him each time he progresses. At this point, he may try to shake his head rather than back up to avoid the pressure. If this occurs, tell him "Quit" and ask again for the back. Always make your commands clear, and always reward him for good behavior.

It is important to stress again the usefulness of voice commands. Each time you ask your horse to back, tell him "back" and repeat the command with pressure until he responds. As he gets the hang of it, his responses should become quicker and easier. He may even try to back without your asking him. This is a sign that he is trying to please you, but you should tell him "No" when this occurs. He needs to learn to respond to the cues and to not try to second-guess you. Gradually, you will be able to wean him off of the pressure and he will respond to your voice alone. This is what you are aiming for.

Your horse may be more difficult than others about backing, and using the pressure point alone may not work with him. If this happens, try using the "gentle whip." The concept is to use the whip as a cue to reinforce the lesson, not to beat your horse until he backs up. You must first teach your horse to yield to halter pressure. Then, take a normal riding whip or crop in your right hand and ask your horse to back with your left hand, applying pressure to the halter and saying the command, "Back." If your horse refuses, tap him on the chest just above the leg connection and repeat the command. If he refuses again, tap your horse on the tops of the front legs and repeat the command. If he refuses another time, increase the intensity of the tap slightly. Work until you get that all-important first step, then praise him. Continue working with this procedure until your horse responds to only halter pressure and voice commands. Remember that when you use the "gentle whip," you are training, not intimidating. Your first goal is to get your horse to back up one step. Don't expect miracles right away.

As your horse gets the hang of it, continue to increase the amount of steps so that he will back until told otherwise. This is accomplished by repetition. The more you work at it, the quicker he will perfect it. Do keep in mind, however, that your horse has a limited attention span. You will get ahead more quickly by working several short sessions rather than by doing one long one. Continue to work until your horse responds to voice commands alone and is backing in a straight line. This will become more important as your training progresses. If you teach the lesson right the first time, it will be easy to transfer to the lunge line and to use under saddle.

The Horse that Crowds

The equine bulldozer is a pet name for the horse that refuses to walk in his own space. Instead, he chooses to plow right over you and walk in your footsteps. Worse yet, he uses his weight to go wherever he sees fit. This is not only aggravating but dangerous. Because the bulldozer doesn't realize or care where you are, he has no qualms about running over the top of you to see whatever he is determined to see. He may also move around blindly and may be prone to stepping over the edge of a hill or path before realizing that there is no longer any footing.

The bulldozer has a very clear agenda. He has no respect for you and is convinced that his wishes are paramount. Do not confuse the bulldozer with the young horse that has yet to learn the concept of direction or with the horse that cuddles you when he is scared. In these situations, patience, training, and slight reprimands will train the horse to walk in his own path. You merely make your direction very clear and let him know that you will still be there if the bogeyman jumps out to get him. The bulldozer, however, must be taught respect and patience. These horses are often demanding and impatient, not to mention difficult to handle.

One of the best ways to temper this impatience is to teach the horse to stand without receiving a lot of attention and without being able to go very far. This tying place is called a "patience tree," but you can use either a tree that is free of debris at the base or a safe tie rack. The point of the lesson is for the horse to stand for fifteen minutes to one-half hour doing nothing but standing tied and learning to be patient. At the beginning, he may try to pace, paw, rear, and generally pitch a fit, but do not be tempted to go over and give him attention. Unless he is in danger of really hurting himself, let him throw his tantrum and learn that all of his efforts will be to no avail. If you do this once a day for about a week, you will be amazed at how patient this horse will become. It will make your ground training infinitely easier, because you will not have to deal with all of his fidgeting while you are trying to train other concepts.

The bulldozer typically is created by a lack of proper handling at an early age. He has had limited exposure to humans, has never been taught respect, and has learned to push his weight around to get what he wants. This horse often does not listen to any commands that you are trying to teach. He is intent on seeing what he wants to see and on doing what he wants to do. The bulldozer is not usually a malicious horse—he is more like a big spoiled baby that has grown up with no manners.

One of the ways to combat the leading problem with the equine bulldozer is to be sure that he is walking in the proper position. This means that whenever you are leading, his shoulder remains even with your shoulder. Teach him this by making him walk up when he begins to lag and by checking him back when he begins to get too far ahead of you. In most cases, the bulldozer will get ahead of you and then try to turn around sharply, cutting you off.

Correcting this habit should take only a firm hand and lots of repetition. It can often be corrected quickly and painlessly. First, teach the horse some patience using a tie rack, then progress to the lead line. Once you have the horse in proper leading position, stay alert for signs that he is going to whirl or try to cut you off. As he starts to come into your space, give the lead two or three sharp jerks and tell him "No" quite firmly. This will stop his forward motion and will check him from coming into you. Start walking again, keeping your hand against his neck and applying pressure away from you and into his path. Make him travel with his head in a straight line with his body. Do not permit rubbernecking—walking in a straight line with his head and neck bent toward you. He must learn to follow his head and be taught to walk in a straight line. Do not allow him to walk ahead of you even a few steps. If he does this, check him back into proper position. When he tries it again, repeat the same sequence. Continue this training, increasing the firmness of your corrections as needed, until he clearly gets the idea that under no circumstance will this be permitted. In addition, do not turn him toward you while you are working on this problem. Instead, turn his head in the direction in which you want him to go and walk around him to make a turn. This correction will force him to stop and turn away from you rather than allowing him to cut into you, and it will make him rely on you to determine his direction. As always, be sure to praise him for correcting himself and walking in the desired track.

The Horse That Lags

The shadow is a horse that consistently trails behind you when you are trying to lead him. No matter how slowly you walk, "the shadow" will walk slower. Bringing him up into proper position may take all the strength you have, and as soon as he gets the chance, he will fall behind like before. The shadow tends to be introverted and timid by nature. Many older Quarter Horses have developed this behavior, probably caused by their previous training, but a young horse that has yet to acquire his sense of confidence can also do this. He will use shadowing as a way to hide behind you and to help him feel protected.

Your horse may have been taught to lead like this. Many owners and riders prefer a horse that trails behind them, and unless the behavior becomes a problem, you may want to leave well enough alone. Your horse may have been ponied off of another horse in the past, and if you think that you may want to pony him again, this previous training may be desirable. Shadowing has its uses. Evaluate your individual situation before you break him of the habit. If you decide that you want to see what he is doing and maybe talk to him along the way, there is a cure.

This horse needs to relearn proper positioning. He must learn to adjust to your speed and be comfortable walking beside you rather than behind you. Use of a simple riding whip may be the answer. As you begin moving forward, put your right hand in front of the horse and keep a short hold on the lead rope. While you give the lead a sharp tug, reach behind with your left hand and gently tap the horse's ribs with the whip. This encourages him to move forward more quickly and positions his shoulder next to yours. Continue to walk, and as he begins to lag behind, tap him gently with the whip. Clucking to him to bring him forward also helps, because many horses have been trained with this vocal cue. Keep repeating the process until he learns that if he travels forward, he will be left undisturbed; if he lags behind, he will get tapped by the whip. He will soon learn that your method of leading is more comfortable for him, and he should oblige willingly. Be sure to let him know when he is doing it correctly so that you can reinforce the behavior. Repeat the drill until he has it down pat.

The end of the lead rope will work if you are semicoordinated and a whip is out of reach. Use it in the same way. With your left hand, reach around with the end of the rope and bump the horse in the ribs. Most of the time it is the sensation rather than the discomfort that will drive him forward.

The Biter

There are two major types of biters. The first is a young horse (most common with stud colts) that uses the nipping to release pent-up energy. This horse is often fun and playful but tends to get very impatient. It is important to be firm with this young horse and to "nip the problem in the bud," but you do not need to reprimand this horse harshly. This form of nipping is actually "Come on, let's play!" rather than "I am going to get you."

The second type of horse is usually more mature and has a history of being abused. He has turned to biting as a protective mechanism and cannot yet differentiate between friend and foe. He feels that all humans are out to hurt him, and he will try to get you before you can get him. This behavior cannot be permitted, yet it can be difficult to rid this horse of the vice completely. Regardless, you should be patient and committed to bringing about the maximum amount of reform possible.

Occasionally you will find a third type of biter. This horse nipped as a youngster, and the previous trainer or handler smacked the horse on the nose as a method of training. This horse has turned biting into a game. He tries to get you as fast as possible, then sees how many ways he can find to avoid punishment. While not being mean, this type of biter can still be destructive. He will also tend to be head shy because of the hit-and-miss game that he has played in the past. Handling about the head and muzzle can be helpful in curbing this evasive response, but be careful that you are not bitten in the process.

Biting is fairly common among horses in the wild, and the reasons why horses use the technique on humans rather than on their equine counterparts can be varied. Most horses can be broken of the habit, but others will be biters for life. The best solution is to prevent and catch the problem at a very early age. The motivation behind the biting and the current age of the horse determine how much reform can occur. Even if you cannot completely break your horse of this habit, you *can* take steps to reduce the problem. This will at least minimize the chance of injury to yourself or to someone else.

When it comes to training your horse not to bite, there are as many tricks of the trade as there are horses that bite. It is impossible to elaborate on all of the ways to decrease biting, so here are some of the more effective methods. When you are working with your biter, you do not turn your back on him when you are within his reach, and never let him "play" with your zipper or the sleeve of your coat. More often than not, this is an entré to a nip. Also be careful when you are grooming any horse that is known to bite. He may be waiting for you to turn your back and may get you where you least expect it. When you are leading a horse that bites, pay attention to where you place your lead hand. Many biters will try to eat your hand as they walk. The biter has perfected the art of biting and then pulling away, and he is lightning fast. Keep your eyes open around this horse or you may end up with less skin than you started with.

When you are training your biter, *never* hit him on the nose. This will inevitably lead to the head-shy problem described earlier. Smack him on the shoulder, on the rump, under the stomach, or even on the jowl, but not on the nose. It will solve nothing and will turn into a battle of the quickest. The best approach is to catch your horse when he is thinking about it but has yet to strike. A sharp "no" or "quit" should make him think otherwise. If he does manage to get in a strike, slap him with the flat of your hand on the neck or shoulder (or on any large body part within reach). Repeat the command "no." Your horse needs to know that you mean it when you warn him. You must be firm and consistent with this horse. There is no room for "I'll let you get away with that one but don't do it again." Be vigilant and reprimand at each and every attempted bite. This especially holds true for the more mature horse that has biting ingrained into his every thought. No matter where he is or who is handling him, do not allow him to bite or even attempt to bite.

Hand feeding your biter is also a no-no. Biting behavior can be exacerbated or even caused by hand feeding treats. We all know that a horse is never satisfied by one treat alone, and his greed will usually lead to a certain amount of grabbiness. The more grabby he gets, the more he will reach for the hand. Out of frustration, he will grab at any hand, hoping that a treat is enveloped in it. If this happens enough, a biter is created. This is not to say that you have to withhold treats. Just be sure to place any and all treats for a biter in the horse's feeder rather than feeding him by hand.

When you handle your biter on the ground, you may need to use a stud chain until the problem is resolved. If you have tried reprimanding him and he still thinks that he can take a piece out of you, this is your next step. When your horse reaches out to bite, yank the chain sharply and say "No." If he tries it again in a short amount of time, yank the chain twice and say "No." Keep increasing the amount of punishment until your horse walks off quietly without trying to eat you. When he performs as you wish, praise him generously. Always give your horse a chance to prove himself between punishments, and always use "No" as your first correction. Give any reprimand beyond that quickly and cleanly, then move on to whatever you were doing. Do not hold grudges. Your horse does not understand that you are still punishing him for something that he did five minutes ago, and he will only become confused and irritated.

Handle your biter as much as possible around his nose and head. Be cautious, but rub his nose, chin, and jowl and let him know that handling can be a pleasurable experience. This will build trust with your horse and will let him know that he doesn't have to be so self-protective around you. While you handle him, stay alert for signs that he may try to sneak in a nip or two, but trust him enough to give him the attention that he deserves. He needs to feel that you are on his side and that he can let his guard down.

Stallions are notorious for biting, and much of it is instinctual. Stallions are born with strong herding and protective instincts. It was up to the stallion to protect the members of his herd and to defend against intruders. Biting was an indispensable weapon in his arsenal. It is virtually impossible to stop a stallion from all nipping, but by giving him respect and handling him properly, you can reduce the tendency dramatically. Be careful not to make it a matter of "me against you." The stallion will react to this attitude and the problem will escalate. This heightened sense of confrontation may even lead a stallion to take a savage approach and cause him to be unruly, especially in his stall or paddock. Instead, take the posture of a friend who has a very clear set of rules—and "no biting" is one of them. The punishment should be an enforcement, not an attack. When he behaves properly, give him lots of love and attention. As mentioned before, *no one* should handle a stallion unless he or she has a complete understanding of horse handling and extensive experience with all types of horses. A beginning handler and a stallion, even if the horse is fairly docile, is a recipe for disaster. If a stallion does turn vicious, he should be handled only by a trainer. Choose a trainer carefully, however, or you could end up with even worse problems.

The Horse That Charges

The sneak attacker is usually a stallion, although other horses occasionally develop this behavior. This horse is very protective of his stall and will literally charge you when you least expect it. Because of the surprise element, this horse can be very dangerous. *Never* turn your back on a horse that is known to exhibit this type of behavior, and always handle this horse with caution. Only experienced handlers should even attempt to reform this horse.

Many horse owners and trainers have a tainted perception of the stallion. They believe that a stallion is always difficult to handle and always bites and that you should get him before he gets you. Most of this thinking is motivated by fear and fueled by horror stories. A stallion is a horse first and foremost. While it is true that you have to be firmer with a stallion because his strong hormonal influences, a stallion should still be loved, respected, and treated with kindness. Contrary to popular belief, intimidation is not an effective method in training a stallion. If you can gain his trust and respect, you will be way ahead of the rest in your ability to train the stallion. Far too many stallions are abused out of ignorance. Train your stallion as you would any other horse. When you handle him, approach him with confidence. He can sense your feelings, and if you are hesitant, he may take advantage of you.

Your chances of reforming the sneak attacker unfortunately hinge on your devoting a substantial amount of time on training, building trust, and breaking down the protective barriers that the horse has built around himself. There are no easy answers to training this horse, and again, it should be attempted only by an experienced horseperson. The training will require you to go all the way back to basics, reteaching him the elements of trust, respect, and willingness.

You will also have to be careful about how you reprimand this horse. If he was previously abused with a whip, use a stud chain to reprimand him, and only punish him the amount needed to get the desired behavior. You cannot lose your temper with this type of horse. He will immediately turn and fight. Patience will have to be the norm, and if you feel yourself getting angry, either restrain your anger or quit for the day. Use punishment very moderately with any abused horse, because all signs of threatening behavior will be looked on as a provocation. Be firm with your commands, make your expectations extremely clear, and follow through with moderation and consistency.

Talking and reassuring are very important in handling this type of horse. Do everything possible to soothe him and to let him know that you are his ally. This horse needs a security blanket that he can rely on, and the more you talk to him, the more secure he will feel. This is a crucial step in reforming this animal, if indeed reform is possible.

The sneak attacker deserves a lot of compassion and understanding, because he was not born mean. He is merely a product of his surroundings. Someone has made him react in this way, and it will take a lot of time to undo the damage. Some stallions may never totally lose that protective wall, but you can take steps to decrease the feeling that they are being threatened.

Don't expect miracles with this horse. You may have to reach a compromise on just how much can be accomplished with him. Take into consideration the age of the horse and how long he was subjected to this type of handling. Perhaps you can decrease the behavior to a tolerable level. With lots of love and understanding, you may win him over and find yourself with a very kind and loyal friend.

Using a Stud Chain

Many people are concerned that the use of a stud chain is inhumane or otherwise unwarranted in any case. A stud chain, in my opinion, has its usefulness in training but *should not be abused.* A stud chain can be used to prevent injury to a handler while veterinary or farrier services are being performed, during clipping, or while handling an excited or difficult horse. It can also be used in loading and lunging. Stud chains are discussed more in later chapters. Keep in mind that the chain is a tool and should *never* be overused or abused. It should be used as a reinforcement of a command but never as an instrument of pain.

Use a chain for basic handling only if your horse may get away from you or if you are handling an excitable horse that may try to whirl, kick, rear, or walk over the top of you. All of these situations may lead to injury. A stud chain often is effective merely by its presence. When your horse knows it's there, he may not even try anything. If this is the case, make him aware of its presence, then leave him alone. If this does not work, give him a simple, quick tug to remind him that you have the upper hand. He may decide to ignore these warnings, which means that you may have to give him several sharp tugs to stop the bad behavior. Just remember that you do have

Proper configuration for a nose chain, which should only be used by experienced hands and with extreme care.

a chain on your horse and that you can do damage if you jerk too hard. Never use a steady pull—only short, quick snaps of the lead.

A stud chain can be used in a variety of configurations. The most common are beneath the chin, over the nose, and under the lip (between the upper lip and the gum). The chin chain is very effective and, under most circumstances, may be all that you need. The chin chain allows you to reinforce your point but stands the least chance of injuring your horse. The nose chain, on the other hand, can damage the cartilage of the nose and the nasal passages if used too harshly. It should therefore be used on a very limited basis or by an experienced trainer only. Occasionally, you may need the leverage of the

Proper configurations for chin chain (above) and lip chain (below). The lip chain should be used only by experienced hands and with extreme care.

lip chain. Vet calls can sometimes warrant use of this chain, because they require great control. The lip chain is similar to a twitch in that it releases endomorphines into the horse's system. These have a natural calming effect on your horse. The lip chain must be used with caution, too, because it can cause damage if used improperly; you may prefer to use a twitch instead. With all chains, it is important to use only as much force as necessary.

Before using a chain, evaluate your motivation. If you feel that you are in danger of losing control of your horse, or if you feel that you could be injured, then a stud chain is useful and sometimes necessary. If, however, you are angry and are looking for a way to get back at your horse, a stud chain is not the answer. Your motivation is to prevent injury, not to cause pain. Abuse occurs when motivations get mixed and emotions enter the picture. You may not mean to harm your horse, but a stud chain in the hands of an angry person can be dangerous.

All horses should be "trained off" the stud chain as soon as possible. In other words, do not rely on the chain as a necessity for the rest of your horse's life. As soon as you feel that you have made progress and that the chance of regression is minimal, go back to a standard lead rope. The stud chain is not a crutch—it is a training device used to create a certain behavior. The only exception is with a stallion. Many (though certainly not all) stallions have been trained with fear as a means of getting them to conform. They have learned to fight back by being nippy or strong-headed. If this has happened for a prolonged period of time, you may always have to handle your stallion with a chain. Do not take for granted, however, that your stallion *must* be handled with a chain. If he is reasonable and has not been abused, he will be fine on a normal lead rope. Except for these situations—to handle a difficult stallion or to train or restrain a horse for a short term—do not use a stud chain. Using caution and a firm hand will produce the same results most of the time, without use of the chain.

Lunging

Lunging is not natural for any horse. As he goes around in circles, more strain is placed on his inside legs than on his outside legs. When he begins to learn to lunge, there will be additional strain on his head and neck from the pressure exerted by the lunge line, and his balance will be altered due to the position of his body. He will also be more likely to make ovals rather than circles, which will cause him to hit the end of the lunge line and be yanked back into a circle. While all of this is a normal process in lunge training, the strain on his legs can be damaging if your horse is too young. It is important to start slowly and easily to build these muscles gradually. Teach the basics at a walk, then gradually increase to a trot. Your very first lesson should last no more than ten minutes. Keep in mind that your horse can get sore muscles just like you can. Do not be tempted to move your horse into a lope or canter too fast. Again, if he is not physically prepared for this, you can cause injury to developing legs and muscles. Your horse should not be lunged at the canter before he is about eighteen months of age, or older for the lighter breeds. If you rush him now, you may be sorry later.

When Is Junior Ready?

The maturity of horses within different breeds varies greatly, and so does the age at which any given horse is ready to begin lunging. As a rule, the larger horse breeds are ready to lunge between ten months and one year. These include Quarter Horses, Paints, Thoroughbreds, Appaloosas, and Saddlebreds. The finer-boned breeds should not be lunged until twenty to twenty-four months. These include Arabians, Morgans, and Shetlands. To determine whether your foal is ready to lunge, be sure that his knees have matured to the point where the strain of lunging will not injure his legs. You can check this by feeling your foal's legs. If you can feel a definite space between the bones in his knees, he is too young to lunge. If his knees feel closed, he might be ready, or you just may not be able to feel the bones. If you have any doubt, wait a little longer. If you want to be absolutely sure, have your foal's legs X-rayed.

Before you jump to the conclusion that your baby is ready to begin lunging, evaluate all of the factors that may affect his training. Is he physically mature enough? Does he have a little muscle tone to begin with, or should he be turned out more to develop muscle tone before training? What is his mental maturity? Is he capable of concentrating on training sessions at this stage of the game, or is he still a gawking baby? Does he have all of his ground-handling basics down pat? Does he respond to voice commands? If, after asking all these questions, there is any negative response or hesitancy on your part, cover some of the other basics first and check him in a month or two.

If you decide to begin lunging him, take it slowly. Work him only at the walk and the trot during the first several months.

Leg Supports

Leg supports are probably the most important tool you can use to prevent leg injuries in your young horse, but they should be used *only* if your youngster has shown that he is prone to such injuries. If you let your young horse test his own boundaries and determine where he should and shouldn't put his feet, you will end up with fewer leg problems than if you pad him to the hilt when he is young. You might end up with a few nicks and scrapes at first but, most of the time, that is all you will find and your horse will figure out where his feet should go. If you find, however, that your youngster is constantly tripping or having trouble with his balance, use splint boots and bell boots for the first part of his training to help prevent serious injury. Remember to wean him off of the splints as his balance progresses. If you don't, he will become reliant on their support, and you will be forced to use them every time you ride.

If your horse is having trouble with his balance and you notice a splint injury on his leg, invest in a good pair of splint boots. They aren't very expensive compared to long-term damage and can save you hundreds of dollars in vet bills and months of lost training. From the time you begin lunge training until the time his balance is developed, your youngster should wear splint boots both on the front and hind legs when lunged and when turned out in an arena after confinement. These will protect him from injuries caused by him interfering with himself, from leg injuries caused by slipping and falling, and from a lot of injuries caused by just plain banging around. As his balance is perfected, he will slip and forge less, signalling you to wean him off of these supports. It should be mentioned that if your horse's splints have a physical cause, such as offset cannon bones or toed-in feet, he may need the supports for a longer period of time, perhaps even for life.

There are many types of splint boots in a wide range of prices. The most expensive are sports-medicine boots. These are tall, padded neoprene boots that have Velcro closures and that extend to the coronet band. They offer the best support to both the pasterns and the lower leg and are well padded to prevent splints. Leather splints are also expensive and, while providing excellent support to the lower leg and fetlock joints, they do nothing to support or protect the pastern. The least expensive are the basic neoprene splint boots that have special padding on the inside of the legs to prevent interference, but they offer minimal support and no pastern support. Expensive does not always mean best. You need to closely evaluate the protection that your horse needs and compare it to the cost of the product. Do not skimp in this area, because a serious injury now could affect your horse for the rest of his life.

Bell boots come in many forms as well. The basic rubber boots with the double Velcro closure are a good choice. The pull-on boots are cheaper, but they will take their toll when you try to put them on. They don't last as long, and the frustration of trying to get them on isn't worth the small difference in price. The more expensive bell boots are used for working horses and are not needed for basic training. You can usually find bell boots on sale or for a reasonable price through one of the catalogs listed at the back of the book.

If your horse has demonstrated a problem with balance in the past, adhere strictly to the use of splint boots when you begin lunge training, but only until his lunge training is complete. The circular motion often causes interference with his front legs and can lead to a nasty splint (an injury that normally occurs on the inside of the front leg from a strike to the bone; it is usually caused by interference from the other hoof). This could set you back in training one to four months. If your horse is reaching too far with his hind legs and is clipping his front feet, add bell boots. This will prevent injury to the front heels and will prevent chipping of his hind feet. The bell boots will also encourage your youngster to pay attention to where his feet are and to how he is using them.

Before you settle on one boot or another, pay attention to how it fits your horse. Bell boots are fairly standard within their sizes, but splint boots can vary widely. Look at the boot on the leg. Does it fit snugly and comfortably? If not, reevaluate the size or style of the boot. Does it seem to offer enough support and protection? If not, you may want to upgrade to a better boot. Keep in mind that the sport boots form to the horse's legs, and it takes three or four sessions for them to mold correctly. They should be adjusted snugly but still allow freedom in the pastern. If you have any questions, do not hesitate to talk to the salesperson at the store or catalog.

Scraping is the most common injury when lunge training is started and is considered to be a normal occurrence at this stage of the game. This injury is caused when the front or hind legs interfere with each other but only in a superficial way. Usually, the only result is the loss of some hide. This minor injury will cause no permanent damage to your horse but will teach your youngster where to properly place his feet to avoid injuring himself.

Clipping is another common injury sustained by the young horse when lunging. Clipping occurs when your horse overreaches with his hind feet and catches the heels of his front feet. Clipping can be superficial or serious, depending on how hard he hits his foot and how far he overreaches. Bell boots are good protection for this type of interference. If he continues to overreach, have your farrier blunt his hind toes. This will make your horse's hind legs break over faster and will thus minimize clipping.

Falling and splinting occur less often but should still be addressed. As your horse progresses with his training, he may often get rambunctious or confused by what is being asked of him and decide to bolt. As he comes in contact with the lunge line and is pulled around in a circle, he may lose his balance and fall. Most of the time, this will only result in a slightly shaken and very embarrassed baby. If this is the case, there is no cause for concern. Occasionally, other injuries will occur. If your horse falls, check his legs and body immediately after the accident. If he is okay, continue the lesson. If he has a leg injury, stop immediately. Splinting can occur after a fall but may not be immediately apparent. A splint feels like a hard lump, usually on the inside of the leg below the knee (see page 5 for a photo of a splint). The splint may be large or small, and your horse will usually not go "off" until the next day. Heat usually is present in the leg shortly after the injury appears and remains for a week or two. Treatment for these injuries is discussed at the end of the chapter.

Getting Started

In addition to splint and bell boots, you will need a sturdy nylon or leather halter, a long lunge line (preferably cotton, because it will minimize the possibility of rope burn), and a lunge whip (about five feet long with a five-foot sash) to begin lunge training. Depending on the method used, you may also need a second lunge line. Later in training, you can use both lines as driving lines for ground driving. You may also wish to get a pair of gloves and a stud chain just in case you need them.

Start your foal in a very small, counterclockwise circle. At first he will be totally confused and may try to turn to face you or turn his rear and try to walk away. Neither can be allowed. If he turns toward you, use your left hand to encourage him forward and your right hand to apply the lunge whip against his rear. Place the whip above the hocks and apply gentle pressure to maintain forward motion. Be firm but patient. He has no idea of what is expected of him and is likely to get very confused. Don't lose your patience and try to force him to do it. He needs to understand the concept before he will be able to progress further.

If your horse is afraid of whips, or you find that he is not responding to this approach, you can try it another way. Attach the first lunge line onto the halter ring under his chin. Attach the second lunge line onto the right halter ring on the side of his nose. Run the second lunge line around the right side of his body, above the hocks, and back to your hands. With this configuration, you will have the front lunge line in your left hand and the body line in your right hand. Gently encourage your foal forward by exerting light pressure on the body line. Do not pull too hard or you will force his head to turn

Beginning lunge training with lunge whip. Notice that the whip is located behind the point of the hip to maintain forward impulsion.

This horse is beginning to lunge using the two lunge line method of training. This is often useful with horses that are afraid of whips.

to the outside, and he will get tangled in the lines. As you ask him to go forward with the body line, use the head line to guide him in a circle. Some horses seem to respond better with this method than with the other. It just depends on your horse.

You must school equally in both directions in order to have a balanced horse. You will probably notice that one side is easier for him than the other. This is normal. Once your horse gets the concept of what you want and you feel that you have drilled him sufficiently on the idea, switch him to one lunge line and the lunge whip. Again, start in very small circles and ask him to walk around you. Use the whip in the same manner as you used the second lunge line. In a short time, he should figure out what is being asked of him.

Do all of this beginning work at a walk, and keep the sessions short in order to retain their effectiveness. Your young horse will have a hard time focusing his efforts for more than ten or fifteen minutes, and forcing him to go longer will only be counterproductive. If you keep his lessons short, he will be able to concentrate completely on your training and will learn that these lessons aren't so bad. Be sure to praise him each and every time he progresses, and while you are working, throw in a healthy amount of "good boys."

Once he gets the concept, you can move on to bigger circles. Release some of the lunge line and keep him going forward by gently popping the whip. If he begins to trot, tell him to "walk" and give a small tug on the lunge line. Repeat this command until he walks. Shorten the lunge line again if necessary, but let it out again as soon as possible. A word of caution: Never wrap the lunge line around your hand. If your horse spooks or bolts, you will be caught and may be dragged. Always give yourself a way out if something happens. Also be watchful of where the lunge line is located. If you find it dragging the ground, take up the slack. A young or inexperienced horse can easily get a foot caught and tangle himself in the line. This will only frighten him and teach him that lunging is scary. You also could accidentally catch one of your own feet over the line and take your legs right out from underneath yourself. This is embarrassing, and the fall may damage more than your pride.

As your horse learns to move out on the lunge line, ask him to trot. Use the command "easy" accompanied by a light tug on the line to keep him slow. You want your horse to understand that there is nothing to be afraid of, and you want to encourage him to move forward at a comfortable pace. Do not allow your horse to rush. Too often, this leads to your horse learning how to use his weight against you, taking the lunge line out of your hands, and running off. If this is already occurring, use a stud chain to keep him under control and to define the boundaries of the circle. If your horse is just thinking about bolting, but not yet reacting, keep moving slowly and smoothly to prevent the problem.

At this point, start work on getting your horse to speed up, then slow down. To do this, cluck and pop the whip, then say "easy" and "here" to ask him to check his speed. This teaches your horse the basics of speed control, and it can be used at any gait. It will also be helpful when you work your horse under saddle. Just give him the concept now. You will work on consistency of the commands a little later.

At this stage, also work your horse on circles of varying sizes. As he gets comfortable with the large circle at a trot, shorten the lunge line and ask him to move in a smaller circle. This forces him to bend at the spine while maintaining forward momentum. A young, untrained horse possesses very little flexibility in his back and spine. Working in smaller circles will help him learn to follow his head and to bend in the direction in which he is moving. It will also add suppleness to his back muscles, something that will be crucial to his training under saddle.

Lefty or Righty?

Once you decide that your horse is ready to lope, you will need to make several evaluations. Horses have side tendencies just like

This horse has learned to lunge and is working properly on the lunge line.

people, and normally they are right-handed or left-handed. This means that they will be more comfortable loping either on the right lead or on the left lead. This is normal. Your horse will often prefer one lead over the other or, when loose, will travel to one direction more than the other. This is important to know, because it will affect your training.

When you work on the lunge line, you must begin to enforce the use of proper leads. If your horse travels to the right, he must be on the right lead in front and behind. Young horses and horses just learning to lunge will not be able to control their balance as well as more mature horses and will have a tendency to "cross-fire," or travel one lead on the front and the other on the hind. If this happens, it is important to tell your horse "no," drop him to a trot, and ask him again for the correct lead. At first, he will cross-fire often, but as his sense of balance and his ability to bend increase, this should occur less and less. If you have done your work with smaller circles at the trot, he should be flexible enough to do a large circle at the lope.

Be sure to keep your work at the end of the lunge line. Loping is difficult at this stage of the game, and asking for a smaller circle is asking too much. Allow your horse to get comfortable at the lope on both leads before you ask him to tighten the circle. If he is still having more trouble on one lead than the other, now is the time to work him more on that lead. Continue to work at the end of the line until the horse moves as freely and easily to the right as he does to the left, and until he is no longer pulling on the lunge line.

As your horse becomes comfortable at the canter, decrease the size of the circles slightly. This may cause your horse to cross-fire again. Continue to work at the smaller circle, correcting your horse until he consistently canters straight again. This will take some time, because you are asking him to become increasingly supple through his back. Small circles force your horse to bend, and at the canter this can be difficult. It may take some time for him to build up the muscles in the loin and back to support these bends. This is understandable and should be expected.

Round and Round We Go

Now is the time to actually work on the circles. By now, your horse may have figured out the circle, and you may not need to work on this further. Other horses have a difficult time working in a circle and will need to have some schooling on this process. If your horse is having trouble, he will do ovals, inconsistent bends, and a multitude of other variations of the basic circle premise. The circles should be smooth and round. If your horse comes in at one end and pulls on the other, work on getting him out on the end of the line on the first end. As he reaches the other end, begin to pull him into the circle before he actually hits the end of the rope. Encourage him to make the turns early. This will assist him in planning his turns and will give him an exact idea of his boundary. To prevent him from coming in too far, flip the lunge whip at his side and encourage him to move back out to the end of the line. Ideally, your horse will lunge in smooth circles just inside the barrier of the lunge line so that he is not pulling on you.

Earlier you introduced your horse to the concept of controlling his speed. Now the concept will be reinforced. At each gait, begin to work on collections and extensions using the command "here" to slow down and "easy" to check any increase in speed. To get him to move out, snap the whip and cluck to him until he speeds up, then tell him "good" for responding correctly. If you introduced these commands before, now you should absolutely enforce them. If you ask him to slow down and he doesn't, give a slight tug on the rope and ask him again. If you feel that he really isn't listening to you, give him a few sharp tugs to regain his attention and ask him again. If you are asking for an extension and he is ignoring you, bring him in a little closer, pop the whip right behind his rear, and ask for the extension again. Keep working until he responds to your voice and collects and extends on command.

As you work on these gaits, pay close attention to how your horse is moving. Look for the ease of the bends and see if he appears to be following his head. If he bends more stiffly to one side than he does to the other, work more on that side. If he is having noticeable difficulty while bending, make a mental note of it and work extensively on bending when you are schooling under saddle or ground driving.

You will also want to do "long and low" exercises with your horse. Encourage him to drop his head and travel with his head below his withers with his nose stretched out. When he does this properly, tell him "good." This exercise will lengthen the back muscles, making it easier for him to become supple and bend when asked. You may also want to feed your horse on the ground until he becomes a little more supple. Again, this encourages lengthening of the back muscles and prevents binding along the spine. These muscles must be relaxed before you can work on building them. Your ultimate goal is to build strong back and loin muscles that will support your horse's movement and create self-carriage.

Another deterrent to building back muscles and bending properly is tension. A young, immature horse can get very tense when working in a large area, especially if a lot is going on outside the arena. His attention is everywhere at one time, and he is sure that he is missing something important. He may become anxious because he is not involved in those activities and may worry that he is not where he is supposed to be. This may produce a nervous horse that will not listen to you, let alone settle down and learn.

You can decrease this tension by using your voice. If you have talked consistently to your horse through grooming and training, he will be accustomed to your voice and it will soothe him now. By reassuring your horse, he will begin to focus his attention on you rather than on activities elsewhere. This will not be an instantaneous change. He will begin to use his ears more and gradually will become more attentive to you. Let him work through this process, and continue to work him even though he may not have completely resolved this conflict within himself. He will learn that no matter what, he will be worked, and he will be asked to listen to you. Eventually, he will learn to settle down and work when he is in the arena.

Drill Sergeant

"Whoa," as you have already learned, is one of the most important commands that your horse will learn, and by now he should perform it properly on the end of a lead line. Now your task is to get him equally proficient on the lunge line. Start at the walk. Let him walk a few circles, then ask him to "whoa." Probably he will either ignore you or will stop slowly. Jerk the lunge line sharply once and tell him "whoa." Now that you have his attention, start him walking again and tell him "whoa." If he ambles to a stop again, repeat the procedure. If he stops immediately, praise him. At first, do this in a short circle for maximum control. As he gets better, allow him to move out on the line but continue to drill him on the command.

When he consistently responds to your command at the walk, move him on to a trot. Again, keep the circles small until he is responding consistently, then move him out on the line. At this point, practice stopping him at varying speeds. Until he is unfailing in his response, do not move on to a lope. You should be able to stop him immediately at both a slow and fast trot before you move on. When he is proficient at this, repeat the same procedure at the canter. By the time you are done, your horse should be a pro at "whoa."

Imprint the gait commands the same way that you did the stop commands. Again, consistency is the key. Ask for a change of gait strongly and clearly, and follow it up with a pop of the whip or a tug on the line if your horse does not respond. His responses should be smooth and clean, and you should not have to ask him four or five times before he performs the transition. If you feel that he is totally ignoring you, sit back on the rope and bring his head sharply to the middle. This should serve to reiterate that you are in control and he is supposed to listen. Once you have his attention back, ask for the transition. He should perform it without hesitation, and if he does, be sure to give him your approval. Continue drilling until you are happy with his progress and feel that he is ready to move on.

At this point, it may be to your benefit to work your horse in a surcingle or bitting rig. This teaches your horse to give down to the bit and will be extremely beneficial when you work under saddle. Bitting rigs and surcingles with side reins vary in design, but all were created to accomplish basically the same goals—to teach your horse to give willingly to the bit and to increase his suppleness. Be sure to choose one that positions your horse's neck at an angle appropriate for his use. In other words, don't use a surcingle that sets the neck high if you are working your western horse. Look instead for a rig that will encourage your horse to travel low and easy.

To use the surcingle with side reins, you will either need to leave his halter on under the bridle or use a lunging caveson (a caveson that has several rings across the noseband and that fits over the headstall). You can also use your regular halter fitted over your headstall with a snaffle bit attached if you plan to ground drive later and want to remove the halter completely. All young horses should be started in a thick, smooth snaffle that has either full cheeks or large rings that will prevent the snaffle from shifting in the horse's mouth. You will need to loosen the halter a little to adjust for the extra bulk of the bridle, but unless your halter is small to begin with, this works fine. Just be sure that the snaffle is free to move and that the halter is adjusted so that it will not interfere with the side reins or with the motion of the snaffle. The bit should be fitted so that it hangs a little in your horse's mouth, encouraging your horse to pick up and hold the bit as he works on the lunge line. This accustoms your horse to the feel of the bit and teaches him to carry it properly.

When you fit the surcingle, be sure that the girth fits snugly around your horse's barrel without any gaping or pinching. This prevents the surcingle from riding up on your horse's withers as he begins to move and exerts pressure on the reins. Allow your horse to accustom himself to the feel of the surcingle before you proceed with the side reins. Introduce your horse slowly to the side reins. This way, he will learn that they will not hurt him and that he can control how much pressure is exerted. There should be a slight amount of tension on the reins, but they should be loose enough so that, as your horse begins to move, he is not truly constricted. At first, he may not want to move forward freely because of the barrier created by the bit. Coax him until he is moving freely at all gaits, and allow him time to figure out that the bit and side reins won't hurt him. He needs to learn that if he puts his head where it belongs, he will be rewarded. As he gets comfortable with the rig, tighten the side reins slightly. Again, allow

Horse with the halter over bridle for lunging with side reins. The snaffle and reins are uninhibited, yet you are able to lunge off of the halter.

him time to acclimate to the reins and work forward freely. Tighten the reins with each lesson until your horse is moving freely on the lunge line and is comfortably carrying his head in the proper position—with his nose slightly out from vertical. This will teach your horse to give down to your hands when you exert pressure on the reins and will decrease the chance of your horse grabbing the bit and running when you begin training under saddle. Be careful not to get the reins too tight. You want to *teach* your horse to give, not force him.

As your horse becomes more comfortable with collection and proper positioning, you will begin to notice a change in his gaits. He will drop his hind end undeneath himself more than he has in the past and will begin to center himself off of his forehand. This is the beginning of "self-carriage." Self-carriage means that your horse is building enough muscle throughout his back and loin to support himself through bends at all gaits. He will become lighter in the forehand and will not need to rely on your hands for support. He will also begin to exhibit more drive from his hocks and hips. While this is only a beginning, it will make developing self-carriage under saddle much easier. It will also teach your horse to balance around corners and in proper position long before he has the added weight of you on his back. To encourage this, allow him to adjust his speed and size of circles slightly in order to acclimate himself to this newly found freedom and grace. Normally this will lead to a more confident, bolder-moving horse. Under saddle, you will have as much trot as you will ever need.

Also encourage length and forward motion at this time. By pushing your horse forward, especially at the trot, you will help him to figure out that he really does have a stride. Lunging over ground poles that are spaced to increase your horse's length of stride will also help his extension and forward motion. As your horse learns to move forward, he will engage his hocks and drop his hind end. This is known as impulsion and should be allowed and encouraged. The more your horse gets his rear end underneath himself, the more he will drive forward and cover ground. He will also learn to free up his front end and will move more easily through the shoulders. Even western and general-pleasure horses should move well and have a ground-covering stride. Length of stride does not mean speed. It is possible to have a low, ground-covering stride without going beyond a jog or lope. Impulsion merely means that the horse is engaging his hocks and is moving freely through the shoulder.

When your horse is moving boldly and confidently on the lunge, progress to ground driving. The benefits of ground driving are numerous. You will teach your horse to give to rein pressure, to follow his head through a bend, and to bend his back as he turns. You will

Young horse learning to ground drive. It is important to keep the horse's attention yet allow him to move and explore without too much hindrance.

also give him confidence as he faces the world without you at his side while still responding to your vocal commands. To prepare for ground driving, put on your surcingle and bridle as you would for lunging. Instead of connecting the side reins to the snaffle, run long lunge lines through the rings of your surcingle and connect them to either side of the snaffle. This makes a modified driving harness. Use a long riding whip or a driving whip to urge your horse forward.

Start by asking your horse to move forward at a walk. If he is confused, tap him on the rear with the whip and tell him "walk." Out of confusion, he may try to turn around to look at you. Using your lunge lines as direct reins, turn him back around so that he is facing away from you and tell him "walk." After a few tries, he should get the idea and take a few steps. You will have to work on this to teach him to continue forward without turning around and looking at you. After you get him moving in a straight line, exert pressure on the right line and ask him to turn to the right. He will probably turn all the way around and look at you. Continue schooling until you can get him to turn both to the left and to the right. Whatever you do, do *not* allow yourself to get frustrated. This is a difficult concept for your young horse to learn, and he needs your patience during training.

When your horse has mastered the basics, ask him to lunge while you hold both driving lines (one will be across his back). Use your lines as lightly as you would use reins. When you ask him to do downward transitions, exert light pressure on both lines while giving him the vocal command to change gaits. Encourage your horse to keep his head in the proper position by maintaining light contact on the lines. You will also want to ask your young horse to back in response to pressure exerted equally on both driving lines, accompanied by the vocal command "back." All of this will take time to perfect but will save you hours of training under saddle.

It's a Wrap

Make it a habit to check your horse's legs for nicks and injuries after lunging. Even some of the best trained horses have fun on the lunge line, and it is possible for any horse to interfere with or nick himself. The use of leg supports will reduce the chance of injury considerably. A visual check should discover any superficial nicks or cuts and should show if your horse has overreached. Other injuries can only be detected if you run your hand down your horse's legs to check for bumps or heat.

Some of the warning signs that may appear after a workout include heat in the leg, swelling, and a lump on one leg that is not on the other. Also be sure that your horse is not "favoring" or limping slightly on any leg. If you notice the head bob that accompanies favoring (a sure sign of discomfort), check your horse's legs and feet thoroughly. The cause for the pain could be as simple as a stone in the shoe, or your horse may have banged himself or pulled a muscle. Check carefully for heat in the leg. This is sometimes very slight and can be detected only by feeling the other leg and comparing their temperatures. Heat is a sure sign that something is going on in the leg. It may only signal slight injury, or it could be a prelude to a more severe strain. Either way, it is important to keep an eye on it. If a serious injury has occurred, it is to your benefit to detect it quickly.

The most common injuries are treated easily, and it is unnecessary to have a vet come out unless your horse is in obvious distress or the unsoundness continues for a length of time without recovery. A rock wedged in his shoe can cause your horse to be tender for a day or two after the rock is removed. Bruising may have occurred, and, in some instances, an abscess may form in the foot. If this happens, your horse will "go off" and will favor that foot. A good farrier can detect the problem and give you sound advice specific to your horse's case. He can also give you advice on helping your horse through recovery from the abscess.

Nicks, clips, and scratches are a normal part of any horse's life, and some horses are more prone to them than others. Unless the nick is very deep, the best remedy is to wash it off thoroughly (preferably with iodine scrub or with a soft soap coupled with hydrogen peroxide) and to apply a topical disinfectant/salve. Bag Balm,® Furazone® cream, Cut & Heal,® and Corona® are all good topical dressings. If the cut is deeper, Wonder Dust® (Farnham) and Wound Dust® (Horse Health) are excellent for blood coagulation and for preventing proud flesh (unhealthy flesh that can invade a serious wound, which, if not removed, will cause permanent disfigurement of the area). Take the time to treat the injury correctly now.

Splints, as you have learned, can also occur from interference caused by lunge training. Splints feel like a hard lump, usually on the inside of the front leg. Your horse may have struck his leg with one of his other hooves, or, occasionally, stress on the leg will cause a splint. Because splints are actually slight fractures, they usually take some time to heal. They should be wrapped for support for the first several days or until the heat disappears in the leg and then should be rested until the leg is completely sound. This can take up to several months, but getting impatient and exercising your horse will only delay recovery. During this time, do not turn out your horse or lunge him except briefly at a slow trot to see if he is sound. As soon as you notice a head bob, stop immediately and put him away. If your horse is in a pasture, you may have to keep his leg wrapped for a longer period of time, and the healing may be slower because of the continuous movement.

Sore muscles can also occur from training and lunging. While not dangerous, they can be uncomfortable for your horse, and serious strains may take several days to heal. A strain is treated with cold water, packs, and wraps. If the injury is in the lower leg, soak the area for fifteen minutes to half an hour in cold water to decrease the heat. Pack the leg with a poultice or clay packing and wrap it. This will keep the heat down and will reduce swelling. The wrapping supports the leg so that your horse will not have to put as much weight on his injury, but take care not to wrap the leg too tightly. Mild strains and muscle pulls that occur elsewhere on the body can be treated by rubbing the area with liniment and resting the muscle. Several good brands are on the market, and most will effectively relieve soreness and encourage circulation to the muscles.

There are several ways to wrap an injury, and, depending on the injury, some are more effective than others. If maximum support and protection are needed, wrap your horse with a "cotton" (several layers of cotton packed together in a slightly stiff wrap that is reusable), and finish with either a standing wrap or, if you are worried about water penetrating the injury, self-adhesive wrapping tape such as Vetrap® (3M) or Guard-Tex® (General Bandages) to secure the cotton.

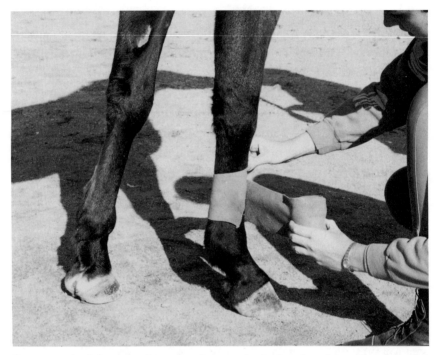

Proper method for wrapping a leg: front to back, keeping the tension firm and constant without inhibiting circulation.

If his injury is less severe and only support is needed, you can use cotton or cotton/polyester track bandages to wrap the leg. Apply the wrap from the outside of the leg to the inside so that the tendon is pulled back into the leg. If you wrap from the inside out, you may cause straining in the tendon. This can increase your horse's recovery time. Apply the wraps snugly but not so tightly that they inhibit circulation. By the same token, if the wrap is applied too loosely, it can pull away from the leg. This provides no support, and the horse could become tangled in the loose bandage and scare himself, causing further injury. Check before you leave to be sure that the bandage is snug and secure. Remember—if you treat the injury properly now, you will spend less time with problems in the future.

Trailering

The Ramp/Step Controversy

There are many benefits in owning a horse trailer, not the least of which is the convenience of transporting your horse immediately in case of an emergency. While many people who own horses do not have a trailer, you should eventually invest in a good, solid, rustfree model if you intend to trail ride with friends, compete at horse shows, ride in parades, or have your kids involved in 4-H.

Shopping for a trailer can be a lot of fun. First you need to decide what size trailer you want. If you only have one or two horses, a two-horse trailer will probably suffice. If you have more horses, you may want a larger trailer. If you will be traveling extensively, you may want to consider a gooseneck trailer with a large dressing room that can double for a camper. Whatever you decide, make sure that you have a vehicle that can safely tow the intended weight, and that you have a hitch that has been welded and bolted to the frame of the vehicle.

Aside from size, you will need to consider whether or not you want your trailer to have a ramp. Many people insist on a ramp, although most horses seem to prefer the step-up type of trailer. There are benefits and drawbacks for each type. A ramp adds pounds to the gross weight of the trailer—weight that you may have to raise and lower by yourself—and it costs several hundred dollars more than a trailer with step-up loading. Many horses do not like the ramps, because they tend to shift as the horse steps up and begins to load. Also, you may encounter loading problems because many horses have been trained to a step-up since birth and are unaccustomed to walking up a ramp. On the flip side, a step-up can be hard on a young horse that has never loaded or on a horse that has a leg or shoulder injury. A panicked horse may hurt himself by backing quickly out of the trailer, not paying any attention to where his feet are landing (although these injuries are often just scrapes). More than anything, the decision is a matter of preference, cost, and what is available at the time you are shopping.

Slant or Straight

When you begin shopping for trailers, many people will tell you that a slant-load trailer is the only way to go. Others will insist that there is no difference hauling with a straight or slant load. Actually, most vets will tell you that hauling a horse with his head facing backward is ideal! Before you decide, explore the options and benefits based on *your* horses, not on the hype of a salesperson.

A straight-load, or in-line, trailer was the norm twenty years ago. The horses were loaded either through the back or sides of the trailer and were positioned in head-to-tail stalls. Limited by this position, the horses shifted their weight forward and backward in response to the motion of the vehicle, with most of their weight moving onto their shoulders. The benefits of the in-line are that they are smaller and lighter in gross weight than a slant, they are much easier to find used, and most horses will haul just fine in them.

The slant trailer was developed about twelve years ago to minimize the stress on the horse's shoulders and to distribute the weight of the horse in a more advantageous manner. The horse is usually loaded in from the rear of the trailer and is angled so that all four legs can be used to balance, and the shifting of weight occurs both side-to-side and front-to-back. The horse is given a little more room to move, and the slant configuration can accommodate a more natural stance. A smaller horse has less problem breathing and eating, because he is not asked to hold his head above a feeder and is able to adjust his head lower to balance his weight.

Because of the adjusted angle and the added space, slant trailers are necessarily larger and heavier than their in-line counterparts, a concession that you may not be willing to abide by. If weight and size are not a concern, and you will be hauling young horses or horses that have had trouble hauling in the past, you may want to consider this option. You will add between three and six hundred extra pounds when hauling a slant, and at least four extra feet of trailer. With this length, it is a good idea to consider a gooseneck rather than a bumper pull to shorten the effect of the trailer, adding turning radius and maneuverability.

If any of your horses have been severely injured in the past or have developed phobias to a trailer due to an accident or trauma, you may have to purchase a slant trailer to keep them safe. Some horses are just not able to deal with the pressures exerted by an in-line or are too confined by the space. The only way to know for sure is to try your horse in the trailer. If he is fine, don't worry about it. If you sense that he is upset or is fussing more than usual when you are hauling him, consider trying him in a slant. The main objective is to find a trailer that fits your needs and the needs of your horses. There are always good new and used trailers on the market, so wait until you find what is best for you.

First Things First

Now that you've found yourself a trailer, or a magnanimous friend who owns one, you are ready to train your horse to go into the trailer.

Before you begin, make sure that the trailer is hitched to your truck. It is dangerous to practice with an unhitched trailer, because your horse's movement can cause the trailer to pitch and roll, which will frighten your horse. This done, wrap your horse's legs in shipping boots or cottons secured with standing wraps. Both are available at most tack stores or from mail-order catalogs at a modest cost. Apply both types of wraps with the fasteners going front to back to ensure proper support of the tendon. Some shipping boots are high enough to protect the hocks on the hind legs, but many times this style annoys the horses more than it protects them.

The purpose of the wraps is to prevent your horse from injuring himself while pawing or scrambling or in case of a sudden stop or turn. Shipping boots should be at least three-fourths of an inch thick with a foam inner core and Velcro closures. Cottons should be a minimum of one-fourth of an inch thick, with the preferred overwrap being a polo wrap (it has more cushion than a standard cotton bandage). This will provide protection against concussion or interference from one leg to another. It will also add some support to the legs, an extra benefit on a long haul. If using polo wraps, however, you will need to check them periodically to ensure that they aren't slipping or binding.

To begin training, you will need a sturdy halter, a long cotton lead, a lunge line, a whip, and a stud chain—just in case. You may also want the assistance of a friend in case things get a little tough. When you begin, work only with the cotton lead attached directly to the halter. Use more force only if absolutely necessary. The point is not to bully your horse into the trailer, but to teach him that there is nothing to be feared by going inside, and that he will get rewarded when he complies. Allow plenty of time for these lessons. You will get frustrated if you have a serious time constraint, and this will only worsen your situation. Take a deep breath and be prepared to exercise a lot of patience.

Environment will play an important role in your trailer-training success. The truck and trailer should be located as far away from noise and distraction as possible. If shade is available, use it. Be sure that the ground around the trailer is free from debris and that the sides of the trailer are clear at least fifteen feet in each direction. Put a flake of hay or a can of grain in the feeder so that when your horse does go in, he will be rewarded.

When you are training, stay as calm, quiet, and patient as possible. Your goal is to teach your horse with a minimum of harassment, intimidation, and force. Anger shouldn't even enter into it. You may only accomplish one step up in the first session, but don't be dismayed. Once a horse is trained properly, you will never have to retrain him again unless he is in an accident or other serious trauma. It is worth the time and effort to do it right the first time.

The Black Hole

Remember the discussion in Chapter 2 about a horse's perception? Now is one of those times when your horse's perception and eyesight can wreak havoc on your training endeavors. Look objectively at your trailer, keeping in mind that horses see in black and white. What you get is a box with a hole in it. Would you jump readily into such a contraption if you had never seen one before? Well, neither would your horse. It is up to you to teach your horse that the contraption will not hurt him and that the world will not come crashing down around him if he stuffs himself into that little box.

In case you hadn't already noticed, horses are a bit claustrophobic by nature and do not like to be confined into any small space where their movement and sight are severely restricted—which is exactly what you are asking your horse to do. If you realize this ahead of time, you will have a little more sympathy and compassion for what your horse will be going through. Keep these fears in mind during training when your patience begins to wane. Horses prefer light-colored trailers over dark ones because they appear less confining. The main point, however, is that in order to get your horse to accept what you are trying to teach him, you must first show him that there is nothing to fear and that he will have to trust your judgment.

Slowly walk your horse up to the trailer and allow him to explore at his own pace. Let him look at the front, the sides, and the back. Don't proceed until your horse has settled down and exhibits a minimum amount of fear when he is in the area of the trailer, and until he will stand quietly next to the back doors when they are open. When you work with the trailer, be sure to keep all escape doors (if any) open so that you will not get trapped, and open all feed doors as well. This will allow more light into the trailer and will create a more encouraging atmosphere for your horse.

Now that your horse will stand quietly next to the trailer, walk him up to the back doors so that he is in a direct line to the open door. If you have escape doors, practice loading on the driver's side of the trailer. If not, use the passenger's side for training, because you can use the driver's side to accompany your horse into the trailer without getting trapped. Stand just inside the trailer door on the appropriate side and ask your horse to come forward. Don't worry about actually getting your horse to step into the trailer at this point. Focus on encouraging him to look at the floor and to explore the back of the trailer. As long as your horse is standing still or is moving or leaning forward, do not fuss with him. If, however, he starts backing away, give him two sharp jerks on the lead, tell him "no," and bring him directly up to the trailer again. After a reprimand, do *not* circle your horse before re-approaching the trailer, because this teaches him that if he misbehaves, he will be able to turn away from the trailer. With this tactic, he has marginally won the battle. Instead, make him continue to face the trailer and walk right back up to it. Work with your horse until he will stand with his front feet next to the step or ramp in a direct line with the opening.

Next, ask your horse to put his front feet in the trailer or on the ramp. Move back into the trailer, keeping tension on his lead rope. Ask him to move forward, but only reprimand if he sets himself

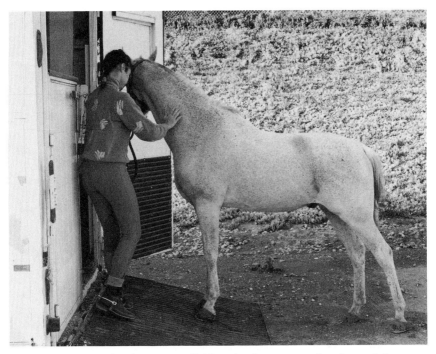

Horse resting quietly after accomplishing the first stages of trailer training.

against the lead or starts to go back. If you have an assistant, now is the time for him or her to move up on your horse and, standing off to one side, place a hand on your horse's rump. This encourages your horse to continue his forward motion. As soon as your horse even sets a foot inside the trailer or ramp, stop and praise him profusely. This is a big step for him, and he must know that he is on the right track toward pleasing you. Continue working until both front feet are in the trailer or on the ramp, then let him stop and gain his bearings.

If, no matter what you do, you cannot get your horse to this point, it is time to try an alternate approach. Tie the lunge line to the center or side bar of the trailer, making sure that the line is at least chest high. While you go inside the trailer and ask your horse to come up

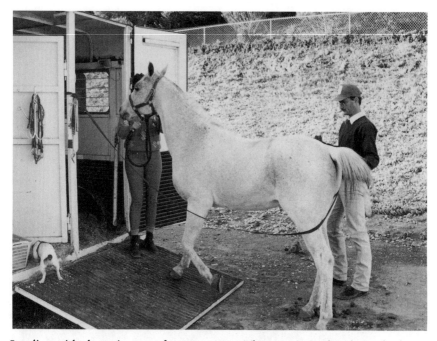

Loading with the assistance of a rump rope. The rope is used to keep the horse moving forward and to position his hips squarely with the trailer.

to the base of the trailer, have your assistant go behind your horse and rest the lunge line across the horse's rear above his hocks. This will act as a rump rope to keep your horse moving forward and to inhibit him from sailing backward against the lead. Use the lunge line to keep him in a direct line with the opening and to keep him going forward into the trailer. If he starts backward, have your assistant use the whip or a hand to slap him on his rump, reprimanding him for his backward motion. If your horse starts to get extremely upset, make him line up to the opening of the trailer, then stop for a moment and reassure him by petting him on the neck and talking to him. It is much more difficult to work with an upset horse, and if you try to do it, you will only add to his fright and confusion. Once your horse has settled down, try again.

Be sure to praise any forward motion and to reprimand any backward motion (unless, of course, you have asked your horse to move backward). Don't be afraid to stop for a breather every now and then. The work that you are doing takes intense concentration by your horse and by all of the handlers involved. If you feel that you have made some progress but all involved are too tired or grumpy to continue, stop for the day and continue the training at a later date. No one said that you have to accomplish the whole thing in one day. Indeed, you will be better off breaking the process down into manageable chunks in order to protect the sanity of all concerned parties, horse included.

At last you will reach the point when your horse will put both of his front and rear feet into the trailer. Should you slam the door and make him deal with it? The answer is a resounding no. Your horse must feel comfortable not only with the loading aspect of the training but also with standing in the trailer. As soon as your horse realizes that he is actually in that contraption, he may hit the reverse and come out as quickly as possible. Don't be dismayed. This is to be expected. Praise your horse for having the bravery to go all the way in, then ask him again to load into the trailer. After several attempts, he will realize that there is nothing to fear inside the trailer, and he will accept standing within its confines. To further encourage your horse, either allow him to eat the hay in the feeder, or, if you are working with a slant load, feed him treats or grain when he stands quietly. This will teach him that if he accepts standing quietly in the trailer, he will be rewarded. When he has stood for a minute or two, ask him to back out and praise him profusely. Repeat the process until your horse will load and unload with a minimum of fuss.

I'm In, I'll Stay In

What happens if you buy a new horse, load him into the trailer, haul him home, then find out that now he is in, there is no way he is coming out? This scenario happens frequently with a horse that has been urged into a trailer but that really has very little trailering experience under his belt. Most of the time, it happens in a two-horse, straight-load trailer where room is minimal, and the horse's fear has caused him to tense. The horse begins to perceive the trailer as a refuge and, out of fear, refuses to back into the scary unknown. This horse probably has never been taught to back at all, let alone back onto a ramp or off of a step. If you find yourself in this situation, review the pressure-point training in Chapter 6 and utilize it to get your horse out. Once accomplished, school your horse extensively on the back command and on loading and unloading before you attempt to haul him again.

Never go into a trailer stall with a frightened horse unless absolutely necessary. Your first step is to use pressure points on his chest to try to coax him out. This failing, run a lunge line from the center divider, across his chest, and out the back to exert pressure and to encourage him to back out willingly. Always use your voice to guide and reassure him, and continue talking to your horse as you work. If absolutely nothing works, you may have to go partially in through the escape door to ease your horse back. If you do this, make sure that you have at least one leg on the outside so that there is no chance of your getting trapped inside.

If your horse refuses to back out, he is doing so out of confusion and fear. The last thing you want to do is to start a battle with an animal that is already confused. This will only upset your horse more and will undoubtedly lead to an unsafe scenario. Instead of losing your patience, understand that your horse truly does not know what you are asking of him. He is frightened of leaving the area that he has found to be safe. Work on soothing the horse until he has quieted down, then quietly work him back out of the trailer.

Scrambled or Well Done?

You will at some point run across a horse that just isn't comfortable with trailering, for whatever reason, and he will move around and scramble from the time you leave home until the time you reach your destination. While "breaking" a horse of scrambling is virtually out of the question, there are things that you can do to reduce the stress on the horse, thus reducing the likelihood that he will scramble.

Many horses scramble at stops and corners, and turning one way usually affects them more than the other. These horses have lost confidence in their ability to keep their feet underneath them, and they work themselves into a nervous sweat by worrying about it. Instead of leaning on the dividers for support, they drop their shoulders, lose their balance, and scramble to regain their footing. They may also spend much of the time braced against the trailer tie so that when you come to a stop, their balance is upset and they have to scramble to get back into position.

A scrambler needs the maximum amount of leg protection that you can give him. A previous injury in the trailer may be the source of his problem, and by protecting his legs from further injury, you will teach him that he can trailer without pain. With this in mind, use cotton standing bandages with the thickest quilted cottons you can find. The cotton will allow his legs to breathe while providing maximum concussion protection. As always, wrap the cotton and bandage from front to back, keeping the tension on the bandage tight enough to prevent slipping en route. Wrap all four legs, then walk the horse for a moment or two to let the bandages settle into place. Recheck the tension before loading to be sure that it is still snug.

When you have loaded the horse, check the trailer ties to be sure that they are adjusted properly. If your trailer ties are not adjustable, don't just use them anyway! Rather, tie the horse with his own lead, making sure that he touches the butt chain or back wall before he hits the end of the trailer tie. This prevents him from having his head in an awkward position, which inhibits him from balancing properly. This is doubly important when you haul a small horse. He will have enough trouble reaching up to the feeder, and by asking him to be tied too short, you are taking away his center of balance and asking for trouble. Instead, allow him more play on the tie so that he can drop his head and move slightly back to spread all four legs for balance. This is where slant-load trailers come in handy—they have hay bags rather than feeders so that the horse can drop his head as needed to balance.

Unless you are only making very short trips, get into the habit of feeding your horse hay while he is traveling. This gives him something to do to prevent boredom and reinforces the concept that riding in the trailer really isn't so bad. If possible, feed a high-roughage, low-protein hay, such as oats or grass, to encourage the horse to eat slowly and remain occupied. If you are hauling in a slant-load, be sure that the hay net or bag is high enough so that if the horse paws or scrambles he will not catch a foot. If you are hauling long-distance, plan stops every four or five hours to walk the horses and to give them water. Most rest areas have quiet areas that can be used to let the horse relax, and water is often available. Bring water with you, however, in case the need arises. Remember that your horse will be eating and probably sweating on the trip and that replenishing this water loss is paramount. Walk your horse for about fifteen minutes at each stop to get the circulation going and to prevent his muscles from tying up.

Driving Tips

The way in which you drive will strongly influence your horse's traveling experiences, and you can prevent undue stress by following a few simple guidelines:

1. Check your truck and trailer before leaving home to be sure that all tires are in good condition and that the vehicles are in solid working order.

2. Check brakes, lights, and turn indicators to be sure that all are working properly.

3. Plan ahead. Know what your route will be, where you are apt to find the trouble traffic, and where you can easily find gas and rest areas that have adequate access and amenities.

4. Make start/stop transitions slowly and smoothly, and avoid stopping rapidly or jerking quickly to one side or the other.

5. Take corners slowly—five miles per hour at most—and make them as wide and sweeping as possible.

6. Avoid rapid lane changes. Instead, signal ahead and take several hundred yards to ease from lane to lane.

7. When in doubt, go slowly. You will get into a lot less trouble if you drive slowly than you will if you go too fast.

8. Keep your eyes open and alert for any signs of trouble down the road, and prepare to brake long before you reach any problems.

Saddle Safety

English Versus Western

In Chapter 1, you learned about the importance of knowing what type of horse you were looking for before you made your purchase. Here is where that decision comes into play. Before you begin saddle breaking your young horse, you want to determine his *probable* usage under saddle. You can then start getting him used to the feel and weight of that particular saddle. If your youngster is long-strided with plenty of forward motion and impulsion, you may want to begin training him English to maximize these talents. If you have a colt that is calm and quiet, that prefers walking around to strenuous exercise, and whose favorite command is "Whoa," you may want to take advantage of his calm demeanor and start him western. In any case, now is the time to make that initial decision—one that is not, by any means, set in stone.

Before you decide which way to begin, consider the following factors, because they will affect your success in any given training. If you are just starting your colt and have done no previous training under saddle with him, you will have no idea how he will react to the added weight of the saddle on his back—let alone with a person on his back. You certainly can watch him at liberty, which will give you an idea about his tendencies and about where he is likely to be most comfortable. You should realize, however, that you may have to change your mind once you get him working under the added weight of a saddle and rider. You may find that the impulsion and stride that you witnessed while he was running free cannot be maintained under saddle, or that he doesn't have the heart, drive, or ability to maintain an English pace for any length of time. If this is the case, consider changing your training to a style that is more suitable for your horse and his abilities.

After you have made your initial decision, and as your training progresses, continue to evaluate your young horse. Pay attention to how his frame changes during collections and extensions, notice his natural tempo and frame on the lunge line, and evaluate his flexibility and suppleness when you progress to ground driving. All of this will give you clues as to what he is most comfortable doing and if he will be capable of performing in the manner you have anticipated. Most important, realize that nothing is absolute. Be flexible and change your plans if you find that your horse is more suitable for another discipline. After all, your purpose is to train your horse into what he will be best at and to utilize most effectively his natural strengths, weaknesses, and way of going.

Hit the Sack

The transition from surcingle to saddle will be easier than you think if it is done properly. Your young horse has already been exposed to the pressure exerted around his barrel by a cinch, and to the pressure on the bridle exerted by side reins, which means that the saddle will seem like little more than additional leather and weight. To prepare your horse for the added flopping that a saddle will bring, use a saddle blanket under the surcingle the next time you take him out to lunge. Place the saddle blanket in the same position that you would if it were being used under your saddle, and use the surcingle to fasten the blanket in place. As your colt begins to move, the blanket will catch the wind and flop on his sides. At first, your horse may spook and try to run off or buck. This is to be expected and, at first, should be allowed. Encourage your horse to get used to the feel before asking him to settle down and work in his usual manner. Talk quietly to him as he accepts the fact that he cannot rid himself of the flopping object on his back.

You can also use blankets and towels to "sack him out" after working on the lunge line. Start by gently rubbing the towel or blanket over the entire length of his body, from head to toe. If you have already done some sensory training on your colt, this part should go smoothly. When your horse is comfortable with this, swing the towel so that it gently hits your horse in the shoulder, stomach, rump, neck, and legs, preparing him for the bumps and movement that he may encounter while being saddled and unsaddled. Progress until he will stand quietly, even if the blanket is swung between his legs, around his head, or under his stomach.

Once accomplished, use the saddle pad and saddle and practice swinging both onto your horse's back, all the while talking quietly and assuring him that nothing will jump out and hurt him. This is bound to be scary for your young horse, because you now have stirrups, girths, and straps flying around in addition to the blanket, and talking to your horse will ease his sense of fear or confusion. Take the time to keep your horse calm, and make all of your movements quiet and unhurried. When you swing the saddle over, set it *gently* on your colt's back rather than slapping it down, and secure the off-side stirrup so that it doesn't flop down and scare him as you swing the saddle over. Once he is used to the basics, you can let some of the other straps, such as the girth and off-side stirrup, swing free and flop around, but not until your colt is comfortable with the basic idea of saddling. Keep in mind that you are not only adding bulk, but weight as well. Go slowly and progress at a rate that is comfortable for your horse.

How's the Fit?

At this stage, it is important that you use equipment that is comfortable and well fitted to your horse. Causing discomfort now will create a training problem that may never be reversed. By making training comfortable for your young horse, you will ensure that you are creating the best possible learning situation, and you will help promote the best results. You will encounter plenty of other problems along the training path, so you might as well eliminate the few that you can.

One of the most common fitting problems occurs at the wither. The saddle should sit comfortably on your horse's back without pinching or resting on the wither itself. Even if the curve of the pommel is slightly above the wither, there will be too much pressure on the wither once you add the weight of the rider. There should be at least two inches between the top of the wither bone and the curve of the pommel. The saddle should also sit comfortably behind the major muscle of the shoulder without actually resting up on the shoulder bone. It is best to first fit the saddle without padding so that you can see exactly where the bars and the front curve of the saddle are resting on your horse. You will also be able to see exactly how much room you have between the wither of the horse and the curve of the pommel. A narrow-backed horse requires a taller, narrower curve, whereas a wide-backed horse requires a shorter, wider curve. To accommodate most horses, allow plenty of height with a moderate width to the curve.

To fit the saddle to yourself, be sure that the seat is comfortable both front and back and that your thighs rest in the narrow part of the tree. If you can feel your thighs brushing the swells of the pommel, or you are sitting closely to the rolls of an English saddle, the saddle is too small. If you have a western saddle with a high back, or cantle, you must allow one-half to one inch more in the seat measurement to accommodate the added height. A saddle is measured from the center point of the tree itself (not the tree with leather already added)

to the center point of the cantle. Saddles are made in half-inch incre-
ments, and if you get a measurement other than this, round down
to the nearest half to allow for the added bulk of the leather on the
tree. Be sure that the saddle is comfortable for you both in length
and depth. You will be spending a lot of time in this saddle, and if
you purchase one that is not fitted properly, it is bound to be a distraction to you and your horse.

Next, consider the length of the saddle itself. Many smaller-backed
horses, like the Arabian and Morgan, cannot accommodate a full-size
saddle and must be ridden with a shorter saddle tree. If you find yourself in this situation, look for a saddle that is marked "Arabian size"
or "Arabian tree" to get a proper fit. You will know if the saddle is
too long if the saddle skirts ride up onto the hip of your horse rather
than fitting comfortably along his back. You will also notice a rub
on each of the horse's hips caused by the friction of the moving saddle.
If not fitted properly, a saddle can make your horse's back very sore,
and saddling your horse can become a battle.

To test the fit of the saddle, ride with adequate padding and get
your horse to work up a sweat. When you take the saddle off, look
for any rub spots or any areas where your horse is dry under the
saddle blanket. These spots show where pressure and friction are causing discomfort. The dry spots are from too much pressure being
exerted on one area, thus preventing the sweat glands from functioning properly. Either your cinch or girth is too tight, or you have
an improperly fitting saddle. Loosen the girth a notch and try riding
again. If the problem recurs, it is because the saddle is too narrow
for your horse, and you will have to find a wider tree. While this
might seem like a hassle at the time, you will prevent a very sore
and sour horse by getting a saddle that fits properly.

Cinch or girth rub is another common problem that can ruin
a perfectly good training session. This happens when a cinch is too
tight or too far forward or backward from the girth line, or when
your horse's skin is sensitive in this area. Whatever the cause, it must

be stopped immediately to prevent further discomfort. Remember—your horse is intelligent. If something hurts him, he is going to do everything in his power to either get away from the source or somehow stop the pain. If his mind is on avoidance, you will find it virtually impossible to have a cooperative training session. Before you buy a new girth, check to be sure that your saddle is fitting properly. Don't be fooled by the old saying that the girth should hang straight from the saddle to the girth area. Some horses just aren't built to allow this. Instead, position the saddle properly and allow the girth to hang a few inches behind the wrinkles of the armpit. If the problem recurs and the saddle isn't too tight, you will either have to get a fleece cover for the girth or find a girth that is wider and that fits more comfortably to your horse's build.

Allow your horse to adjust to the added weight and pressures of the saddle and girth before you attempt to climb on board. A young or untrained horse's sense of balance is not yet fully formed, and you must let him rediscover his center of balance before you attempt to add any other weight. Your horse now has more on his back in the way of equipment and bulk as well. The sheer bulk of a saddle will feel significantly different to him than the surcingle did, and stirrups will be flapping around to boot. Don't be afraid to take your time and provide a period of adjustment before you ask your horse to cope with anything more. By allowing your horse to realize that this is just another step in the process, you can prevent yourself or your horse from getting unnecessarily injured, and he will maintain a happy, willing attitude for learning.

Strap Check

Before you continue, check the wear and pliability of the leather on your saddle. If the saddle is older, some of the straps may have become dried or cracked, lessening their flexibility and safety. Before you attempt to train with your saddle, make sure that all of the leather

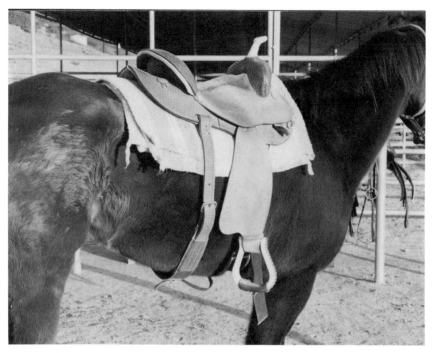

Proper adjustment of a regular back cinch.

is in functioning order and that none of the major straps show cracking or splitting. If they do, replace them. You are working with an unpredictable animal and are trusting your safety to the sturdiness of your equipment. Be sure that your trust is warranted before you begin training.

If you are working with a western saddle that is equipped with a back cinch, check the adjustment of this cinch. If it is too tight, it can act as a bucking strap and can actually encourage your horse to buck. If it is too loose, your horse could catch a hind leg in the strap, entangle himself, and fall. Neither scenario leads to productive training. Adjust the strap so that you can place three fingers vertically between your horse's stomach and the strap. If you will be riding a roping or working horse, make sure that the back cinch is significantly wider, that it is padded, and that it is fitted a bit more snugly.

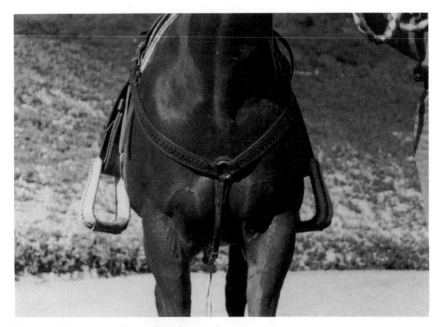

Proper adjustment of a regular breastplate.

If you will be working out on trail and will be consistently going up and down hills, you may want to add a breastplate to stabilize the saddle and prevent friction rubs. The breastplate should rest at the base of your horse's neck and will attach to each side of your saddle. You also want to use a connecting strap that runs from the center of your breastplate, between your horse's front legs, and down to a ring on the girth. This prevents the breastplate from riding up too high on your horse's neck. Adjust it so that it fits snugly against your horse's chest but still allows freedom and mobility through the chest and shoulder.

Preliminary Precautions

When you decide that it is actually time to tighten the girth fully, do it in stages. Take the girth up so that your saddle is somewhat secure but not tight, and walk your horse around for a few steps. Then take the girth up another two notches. Again walk your horse. Continue this procedure until you feel that the saddle is snug but not overly tight. By using this method and taking a little extra time, you will prevent your horse from becoming "cinchy," or reacting to the girth being taken up too quickly because of the pain and discomfort it causes.

Some horses have already been programmed to react to saddling and cinching. They may have been injured in the past or may be sensitive to being cut in half by someone trying to cinch them up all at once. If this has occurred in the past, your horse will react strongly if you try to cinch him up without allowing him time to adjust. Your horse may rear or pull back violently to get away from the pressure. If you sense that this is going to be a problem, be sure that the horse is tied lightly so that his release, should he pull back, will be immediate, but make sure that you maintain control of the lead. It is important to let your horse know that you will not hurt him and that even if he pulls away, he will not get loose. With time and some humane cinching, you will be able to minimize, if not eliminate, this reaction to saddling and cinching.

Now is the time to evaluate if your horse will need leg supports or protection, such as splint or bell boots, while he is adjusting to the additional weight of the saddle, or if he is coordinated enough to do without them. As a rule of thumb, your young horse should be allowed to work without splint boots unless he has shown a tendency to interfere or clip himself when lunging. By allowing a young horse to learn where his feet are and how he can control them, you can virtually eliminate the chance of splints occurring from interference later in life. If, however, your horse has already been injured or tends to interfere, protect him adequately until he becomes accustomed to the weight of the saddle and to the change in his center of gravity. At that point, you can remove the supports. As discussed in Chapter 9, if you constantly have protection on your young horse, he will never really learn where his feet are going and will constantly bump and interfere with himself, causing splints and other injuries. A few bumps early will teach him to watch where he is going, and you should encounter fewer problems when he gets older.

Once you reach this stage, you may be very tempted to just hop on and ride off into the sunset. A word of caution: It won't work that way, and you will almost certainly end up on your rear end with your horse running off into the sunset. Now is not the time to cut corners in your training. Instead, you must become hypercautious to protect both you and your horse. You are introducing a multitude of new concepts to him, and he may decide to react to the smallest of excuses and pitch a fit. Unless you have trained other young horses extensively in the past, let a professional take your horse from the groundwork stage to performing under saddle, at least until your horse is green broke or will perform with some comfort at the walk, trot, and canter or lope.

Getting On

This chapter contains some of the most advanced information in the book. Attempt this training only if you have handled many types of horses, from young to old, for several years. This chapter, and parts of Chapter 13, are for experienced riders only—people who have done just about everything but start their own horse and who finally want the basic information that they need to do so. If you have any doubts about your ability to follow these procedures, relinquish this responsibility to an experienced trainer.

Weights and Measures

You have one last consideration before you progress with your horse's training—how the combined weight of yourself and your equipment will affect your horse's balance and how you can minimize the effects of these factors. Although your horse has had a chance to adjust to the added weight of the saddle and has learned to alter his position to compensate for that weight, there is very little you can do to simulate the weight that your body will add. It is therefore important to take the next training sessions very slowly and to progress at a speed that is comfortable to both you and your horse. At times you will think that the training suggestions are too conservative. Every step

173

outlined has been proven to be effective in breaking the young horse, and each is a vital element to your success. Do not be tempted to cut corners or to "speed things up," because you will only end up losing time in the long run.

Before you decide that your horse is ready to start this process, put him out on the lunge line with the saddle on his back and observe his mood. Is he relaxed or upset? Is the weather conducive to effective training, or is it cold and windy and liable to create lots of distractions? Has your horse had any recent medication that might make him grumpy or uncomfortable? Watch your horse's moods carefully while you are lunging him to see if he is in the proper frame of mind for such a big step. The bottom line is to evaluate the day, the environment, and the mood of yourself and your horse before you decide that today is the day to begin.

A Step Up

If your decision is yes, you need to do a little more groundwork before you start the training. To be successful with this training, it is crucial that you work with a competent header—someone who you trust and who has had solid experience in working with horses—and to work in an enclosed area where you will have your horse's attention. Again, *always* lunge your young horse before you attempt any type of saddle work. Your baby has an overabundance of energy and an extremely short attention span. He needs to be able to get out and kick up his heels before he settles down to a training session. Skipping this step is one of the quickest ways to get hurt. You need to understand your youngster's vitality and allow him to get some of the bucks out on the lunge line so that he isn't tempted to take them out on you, and he needs to warm up those muscles to prevent strain from overexertion.

After lunging for fifteen minutes or so with your horse saddled and bridled (with a snaffle or bosal of course), have your header stand at your horse's head. One end of the lunge line is connected to your horse's halter, and the other is in the header's hand. It is easier if you put the bridle over the halter for this training, but it will work either way. Just be sure that the reins are not limited by the halter or the lunge line. Check the girth to be sure that it has not loosened, and if it has, tighten it so that the saddle is snug.

Standing on the left side of your horse, reach up and grab the left rein in your left hand and the right rein in your right hand. Make sure that the reins are not twisted and that they are lying smoothly on your horse's neck. With your hands on either side of your horse's withers, reach across with your right hand, exert equal pressure on the reins, and ask your horse to give to the bridle. At first he may, out of confusion, raise his head. Tell him "no" and again ask him to give to the bridle. Continue the process until he understands and drops his head down when he feels the pressure (as he was taught to do with the side reins), and until he stands quietly with his head down. Tell him "good" and pat him on the neck. Repeat the process several times until he is performing correctly and consistently to the pressure. This drill is the basis for yielding to your hands and giving to the bit and is crucial for your control once you get on.

Your header is there as a safety precaution only and should not be relied on to be the one in control of your horse. Never allow your reins to go totally slack while you work your young horse under saddle, and rely on your header only in an emergency and as an additional safety measure. It is your responsibility to stay in control of your horse at all times, which means that you *must keep control of the reins*. This will be explained in the discussion on mounting, but it is important that you keep this rule in mind as you work.

Another important rule is that you must constantly be prepared to get out of your horse's way in case he becomes startled. This means staying light on your feet and being aware of your horse and your surroundings. Paying attention to signs from the horse himself (laying back of his ears, tightening of his muscles, darkening of his eye) and

Horse yielding properly to the bit. If you practice doing this every time you get on, you will never have a problem with your horse walking off as you swing up.

being aware of happenings outside of the arena can help you avoid a potentially dangerous situation. If you hear commotion, stop what you are doing and look around to evaluate the situation. If your horse becomes startled, you don't want to be standing up in the stirrup or caught in a dangerous position. This is one of the few instances where you should allow your header to keep control of your horse while you focus on getting out of the way.

Pogo Stick

The next lesson involves "the art of bouncing," and you will use it often through the next few steps. Essentially, you are testing your horse's reaction to movement and weight before you put yourself in a precarious position. While your assistant holds your horse, put your hand in the stirrup and exert weight downward in a bouncing motion. During this process, talk to your horse, telling him "whoa" and "good boy" to encourage and calm him. Repeat this process on the other side, and alternate sides until your horse stands quietly every time you put weight in the stirrup.

Next, gather up your reins in your left hand, and place your left hand on your horse's withers, just in front of the pommel of the saddle. Make sure that your reins are taut enough to have control but not so tight that they interfere with your horse. Put your right hand on the cantle (or back) of the saddle, and slip the ball of your left foot into the stirrup. Bounce several times to check your horse's reaction and to gain momentum. Then, without using the saddle to pull yourself up, stand up in the stirrup. Do not swing your leg over yet, and do not poke your horse in the stomach as you go up. Try to make the motion as smooth and quiet as possible, and make sure that your header has firm control before you go up. Place your right hand in the middle of the saddle for support, and keep your left hand (with the reins) fairly free so that if you need to control the horse yourself, you can. If your horse responds quietly, bounce your weight in the stirrup to accustom your horse to the movement and weight that he will feel while being mounted and ridden. If he stays calm, repeat the procedure on the off-side. If your horse becomes frightened or begins to move suddenly, step down immediately and get control of him. Once he is calm, try again. If your horse goes into a panic or appears extremely frightened, consider getting a trainer's assistance.

If your horse responds well, proceed to the next step. Keep in mind that all work should be done from both sides of your horse. This training will come in useful if you get into a situation where you must dismount quickly and cannot afford to startle your horse. If he is accustomed to being mounted and dismounted on the off-side,

The first stage of breaking. Both the rider and header are quieting the horse and the rider is maintaining control of the reins at all times.

he will not be frightened if you have to use this unconventional mount or dismount.

Now that your horse is comfortable with the beginning stages of mounting, see how he reacts to weight and movement across his back. Approach your horse as before, but this time when you stand up in the stirrup, continue over until you are lying across your horse's back. Be sure that only the ball of your foot is in the stirrup in case you need to step down quickly, and keep your left elbow underneath you until you are sure that your horse is quiet. Also stay alert for signs that your horse is thinking about spooking or bolting.

While lying across his back, pet him on the hip, the side, and the shoulder, and talk to him continuously to let him know that it is only you up there and not some alien. You need to get your horse accustomed to hearing your voice from above him rather than from

Second stage of breaking. After carefully lying across your horse's back, touch him over his entire body to accustom him to the feel while reassuring him with your voice.

the ground, so use this opportunity to start vocal training. After your horse's initial shock wears off, move around in the saddle to accustom him to movement as well as to the weight on his back. Use your hands to touch and pet your horse everywhere you can reach, from his neck and head to under his stomach and around to his croup. Work in this manner until you are confident of your horse's reactions and until you feel that he is comfortable enough for the next step.

Don't Throw Caution to the Wind

Let's take a break in the action to discuss some concepts that are important to this type of training. As you reach this stage and things are going smoothly, you might find yourself getting just a bit cocky — thinking that you are the world's greatest horse trainer and that you can tackle anything. While having confidence in yourself is crucial, becoming overly confident can lead to injury. You are working with a living, thinking animal that will not always be predictable. Even the most trained horse can become startled and act irrationally, so imagine what may happen with your young horse. The spark that sets him off may be totally invisible to you but may be just the impetus that he needs to pitch a fit. As soon as you feel yourself getting just a little cocky, think back to the last time you were unexpectedly bucked off or were caught by a flying head or hoof. If you have any doubt about your infallibility, I have a stack of doctor bills that I will be happy to send you as a reminder.

Your motto should be to remain cautious and stay aware. Many injuries can be prevented if you stay on your toes and pay attention to what is happening around you. It is easy to get so entranced by training that you forget about the world beyond the arena fence. Although intense concentration is sometimes needed, tunnel vision can easily get you hurt. Even if *you* are not concentrating on what is going on, your horse most certainly is. His eyes and ears are working at all times, and he will catch any commotion as it begins. If you are oblivious to these happenings, you could get run over before you knew what hit you. This awareness should extend to your header as well. Your assistant is there to protect you and your horse, and if you are in a position where you cannot fully focus on your surroundings, your header must become an extension of your eyes and ears.

Your header is the one person who you will want to choose with great care. A competent, alert header will make your job go more quickly and smoothly than you ever could accomplish on your own. By keeping your horse calm and preventing him from getting into a full panic, your header can make your horse's memory of the training a positive one. Your header must be confident in his or her abilities to handle a frightened, confused horse with skill and be able to maintain control if your horse tries to bolt. The header can also alert you to changes in your horse's demeanor that could affect your training. If your assistant senses a darkening of your horse's eye that precedes a tantrum, you can be informed and can act accordingly. If your horse is kept close to the header's side, he can be stopped from bolting before he ever gets the leverage to pull away. If you treat your header with respect, he or she will become your partner in training and will increase the effectiveness of your lessons while reveling in your successes. Most importantly, this person can keep both you and your horse safe during this fragile transition period.

Earlier, several warning signs were mentioned that can signal that your horse is contemplating action of his own rather than going along with what you are trying to teach him. These include hunching his back, trying to turn and bite, cow kicking to the side, bunching his feet to prepare to jump or bolt, dropping his head, side-passing, and throwing his head. Any one of these should be evaluated carefully to determine if you or your header are in danger. While much of his planned behavior is a mild rebellion, a horse with a naturally explosive personality can turn even the simplest of training sessions into World War III, with you as a casualty. If you sense that this type of explosion is about to occur, or if your horse has shown a tendency in the past to deal with confrontation explosively, consider getting professional assistance to work him through this problem.

That First Big Step

Assuming all has gone smoothly and your horse is progressing willingly and calmly, you are ready to continue. The next phase will be either exhilarating or frustrating, depending on your individual horse. If all progresses as planned, your first ride while astride your horse can be one of the most memorable days in your training. However, if your horse has an attack of total regression and loses control when you swing over, you will have to go back to the beginning and start again—a backslide that will, without a doubt, frustrate you. If this occurs, keep your chin up and don't allow yourself to get angry or impatient. Your horse isn't doing this on purpose; he merely cannot cope right away with what you're trying to teach him and will need more groundwork before you attempt this training again.

As you may have guessed, the next step is to actually swing your leg over and sit on your horse's back. More than ever, take care to ensure that your horse stays calm and quiet and that the entire experience will be a pleasant one. Perform all movements quietly and with care to avoid startling your horse, and eliminate any excessive movement. Take a deep breath before you start and concentrate on staying calm and in control.

As before, stand up in the stirrup, keeping your left hand on your horse's neck with the reins. Your right hand supports your weight on the saddle. Your header should be constantly talking to your horse, reassuring him while still keeping a tight hold on the lead rope. Stand for a moment in the stirrup, then quietly swing your leg over your horse's back, taking care not to bang him in the rump with your leg. Settle your weight on your horse's back. Pick up your off-stirrup and be sure that your seat is nice and deep. Now join your header in reassuring your horse by petting him on the neck and saying "good boy" and "easy."

When you feel your horse start to relax, wiggle around in the saddle to create some subtle movement on his back. If he starts to panic, immediately stop the motion, take up on the reins while your header pulls back on the lead, and tell him "whoa." Calm him down for a few moments, then try again. When your horse learns that this motion will not hurt him and that it is only you moving around on his back, increase the motion to include your legs, your arms, and your upper body. Move your hands so that you are petting your horse over every inch that you can reach, from tail to ears, all the while reassuring him with your voice. Swing each leg so that it gently bumps him on the shoulder and stomach to accustom him to the feel that a rider will make while riding. Shift your weight back and forth between your left and right stirrups to simulate the feeling of mounting or adjusting the saddle once mounted. Do all of this while your header pays close attention to your horse's reaction and watches for signs of trouble.

Now, more than ever, you will be required to rely on the judgment of your header, keeping in mind that you are still the one who is ultimately responsible for controlling your horse. Don't get so carried away with petting and playing that you forget to maintain control of your horse's head. It only takes one time of being caught off guard to learn your lesson. Because you are on the horse's back, you have the most control and leverage. If your header should trip, fall, or have the rope ripped out of his or her hands, you are the one who can stop your horse. Your header will, however, be basically in control of where your horse is going. Your horse is more comfortable being led than being ridden, so he will respond more easily to the turning and stopping cues of your header. Gradually, he will learn to accept the bit and reins, as well as your legs and seat, as his cues, but right now he will accept what he is most comfortable with—the cues from the ground.

Ask your header to walk your horse a few steps and then stop. Because of the added weight on your horse's back, he may be a bit reluctant at first to move forward. Continue to urge him on, both with your legs and with the lead, until you get those all-important first steps. Praise your horse for responding correctly and for being so brave. To him this is scary stuff! Again ask your horse to move forward, increasing the amount of leg pressure and decreasing the amount of header control. When he responds correctly, praise him generously. Also ask your horse to back by giving vocal commands, and have your header give pressure commands. Take up lightly on the reins yourself, but avoid putting so much pressure on the bridle that backing turns into a battle. Instead, focus on teaching the *concept* of backing. You can clean up the response later. When your horse moves forward with only cues from your legs, stops primarily from

Third stage of breaking. This horse is taking his first few steps with a rider on his back. Notice the position of the header and the control he has on the horse.

rein pressure, and backs at least a few steps by mutual effort, stop the lesson, get off, and praise him.

All of this training must be done slowly and positively to gain lasting effects and to keep your horse looking forward to his training sessions. Praise is more important than ever because your horse is feeling tentative and unsure of himself, and he needs to know when he is performing to your satisfaction and when he is not. While you are training, rebuild his confidence and let him know that he really will be okay and that you have all the faith in the world in his abilities. This reassurance becomes increasingly important as you progress. The more confidence you can give him, the quicker he will accept his new situation and try new things. You are his only stability right now, and he needs to rely on you for consistency and praise.

At the beginning of every training session, and after you have lunged your horse to warm him up and get the bucks out, do a brief review of the previous lesson, just to be sure that your horse has not forgotten anything. This takes only a few minutes and puts your horse in the proper frame of mind. Keep him on the lunge line while you continue your training so that you can promote his independence while you still maintain control in case something happens. Once you have your horse moving forward on leg pressure only, ask your header to step back from your horse and allow some slack in the lunge line. This puts your horse in an independent situation where he will be forced to listen to your cues and direction rather than relying on your header. If he tries to stop, gently put your legs on his sides and encourage him to continue walking. Gradually increase the distance from your header until you are well out on the lunge line. Talk to your horse most of the time that you are on his back to soothe him and to reinforce your vocal cues.

When your horse appears to be walking calmly, ask him to stop by putting light pressure on the reins and telling him "whoa." He may take a few steps to respond, but any proper behavior at this stage should be praised. Take a few minutes to pet and reassure him, then ask him to move forward again by squeezing your legs, clucking, and telling him "walk." If he responds correctly, praise him. Continue stopping and starting for several more times, then change direction.

To reverse, use your inside rein to encourage his head to the bend and your outside leg to reinforce the turn. Make sure that your header takes up on the line slightly so that it does not drag on the ground. It could be very dangerous for your horse if he gets his leg caught. Always be sure that your header, while not maintaining steady contact, keeps the lunge line from dragging on the ground to prevent spooking or entanglement. Practice stopping, starting, and reversing for the rest of this session, making sure that your horse responds to bit pressure and that he follows his head through the bends. At the end of the session, use rein pressure and the vocal command "back" to ask your horse to back a few steps. If necessary, use your header to get your

Now you can move out to the end of the lunge line. The horse is concentrating but not resisting the rider's aids.

horse started, but ask your horse to respond primarily to your subtle rein pressure. If he starts to throw his head or resist the pressure, tell him "no" and give him two light bumps on one rein, then ask him again. Repeat the process until your horse understands and backs a few steps with you in command.

Wait For Me!

Well, you've done it! You've taken your first solo steps. Congratulations on a job well done. From here, you can *slowly* build your horse's confidence at the walk and the jog until he is ready to be taken off of the lunge line. You will know when the time is right. Your horse will be comfortable with carrying your weight. He will follow his head while cornering and will control his speed with consistency. Both of you will be excited to venture out on your own.

But don't get carried away. Your horse is a long way from being broke. As a matter of fact, your breaking has just begun. Training your horse under saddle will take months to accomplish, and even then, your horse should always continue to learn new things. Don't be tempted to throw caution to the wind and rush through your future training. Nor should you try to take your horse out of the confined area in which you have been working. Too many variables are still at play to risk that courageous leap just yet. The lessons that your horse learns now will set his basics for the rest of his life. It is more important than ever to take one day at a time, one step at a time, and ensure that your horse has a complete understanding of the concepts that you are teaching before you move on.

Now you can move your horse into a jog or trot on the lunge line. Once you feel that he is ready, take him off of the lunge line and work on your own until your horse performs both of these gaits quietly, confidently, and easily. Always enforce proper leg yields and rein commands during these sessions. Start subtly, then reinforce the command. In other words, ask your horse to turn off of your leg commands, and if he doesn't respond, increase the leg command and use your reins to insist on the turn. After your horse learns what is being asked, praise him when he obeys and reprimand him when he ignores you. Reprimand him with a solid bump of your heel or with a bump from the leading rein. Always ask your horse again for the movement to allow him to correct himself. If he performs incorrectly, reprimand him and ask again. Continue this cycle until your horse performs off of the subtle cue that is being given.

The same holds true for him standing still while you are getting on. Remember, "whoa" means to stop now, not four or five strides later. Whenever you mount your horse, take up on the reins with your left hand for control, and use your right hand to assist yourself up. If your horse starts to move forward, stop when you are in the "standing-in-the-stirrup" position and correct his forward movement by pulling back and saying "whoa." Make your horse stop before you continue mounting. If he has a habit of walking off, practice mounting and dismounting while you correct him until he stands quietly when you mount. As always, enforce the command "whoa" unmercifully. It is the most important command, both on the ground and under saddle.

As you work your horse on walk, jog/trot, and leg yields, you can accomplish a multitude of other training lessons. Instead of doing just straight lines and circles with your horse, try doing serpentines (patterns that look like snakes with a series of bends), turns around barrels, or figure-eights. All of these movements encourage your horse to bend, to follow his head, and to change direction. If you use your legs properly, with your inside leg supporting the bend and your outside leg cuing the turn, these important basics will become ingrained in your horse and you can incorporate all of them into your future training. A proper bend teaches your horse to follow his head, to bend through his entire body, and to keep his back supple. This flexibility will be useful when you teach collection, drive, and impulsion.

When your horse is confident and is traveling in a balanced and cadenced manner at the walk and jog/trot with proper submission to the bit, put him back on the lunge line and work on the canter/lope. Do this training in the same manner as you did for the walk and jog/trot. Be careful, however, to enforce proper leads and to keep balance problems to a minimum. Do this by staying quiet on your horse's back (don't try to throw him into the canter/lope) and by keeping your hands constant and still. Take extra care to keep your hips square and your body upright, leaning neither forward nor backward, when you ask your horse for the gait change. Keep your hands low on your horse's neck, and maintain constant, *light* contact with your horse's mouth. Your horse cannot begin to work in a balanced manner if you are constantly wiggling around on his back or banging

This horse's back feet are following the line of her front feet and her entire spine and neck are bent in line with the arc. This is a proper bend.

his mouth with the bit. When he is comfortable on the lunge line, take him out on the rail by himself and progress from there.

It is very important that you resist the temptation to rush your horse. By now, his mind is swimming with new lessons, commands, and concepts, and he is a bit overwhelmed with all that is being asked of him. He needs several weeks or even months of drills to eliminate this sensory overload. Don't ask him to progress further until you have drilled the previous lessons so extensively that they are almost second nature to him. Allow him a period of adjustment after each hurdle to accustom himself to the new skill, knowledge, and physical capability that he has acquired. You will have to work him through periods of rebellion, frustration, and sore muscles before he truly understands the lessons and can perform them easily. Don't rush the process to achieve instant gratification. Focus instead on the long term and on having a happy, healthy, well-trained horse.

Tough Stuff

The information in this chapter deals with problem horses, and most of it is geared toward more experienced horse handlers. The problems discussed here are beyond the norm in horse training and vary in their severity. Only attempt the suggested reforms if you have handled problem horses in the past and are confident in your abilities. A problem horse can be dangerous, and unless you can somewhat predict what these horses will do (an intuition that comes with years of handling), don't attempt to reform these horses yourself. Put them in the hands of a competent professional. If you have any doubts, do not take the chance. If you are comfortable with attempting the reform, study the following information on how to predict, recognize, and solve most of these problems.

The Horse That Pulls Away

If your horse has been abused or has accidentally learned to pull away and has made it into a habit, you could end up with rope burns that range from mild to severe. Your horse has learned to use his weight and size to leverage against you and tear the lead or lunge rope out of your hands to gain his freedom. He may only try it while lunging or, in more severe cases, while you are leading and least expect it. Once loose, he may put himself in a dangerous position—and he will not be easy to catch. The big temptation is to punish your horse harshly once you catch him, but all this really teaches him is that he will get in trouble when you catch him and therefore he needs to avoid you. Instead, catch the problem when it occurs and reprimand your horse before he is able to pull away. This way, you are treating the problem and not the symptom.

Before your horse attempts such an action, he will most certainly tip you off in some way. If you know that he is prone to this behavior, stay hyperalert until you have trained him out of the problem. Watch for signs, such as when he bunches his muscles, swings his head, pins his ears, slows down or speeds up, or swings his hips out of leading position. If he displays any of this behavior, prepare to have him try to pull away. It is important not to overreact to these signs, because there may be another cause, and you want to catch him in the act and allow him to begin the action before you reprimand. Be prepared to react in a split second to catch him as he begins to pull away. That is when your reprimand will be most effective, and it will clearly signal to him why he is being reprimanded.

Use a stud chain with your horse, along with a pair of solid leather gloves, until this problem is remedied. The chain increases your leverage and puts you on equal ground with the strength of your horse. The gloves prevent rope burn and help to keep the rope from shifting in your hands. When possible, use a cotton lead or lunge line for this training. It is easier on your hands and will not get quite as slippery as the smooth nylon ones will. Also check your halter to be sure that it is in good shape, that it fits properly, and, if it is leather, that it has no weak spots.

Because your horse can brace against pressure under his chin, the most effective configuration for the chain is over his nose (see the photo on page 125). As he begins to pull away, the chain puts pressure on the bridge of his nose, urging him to drop his head and give to the chain. By the time you feel pressure on the lead, he will have moved far enough away that he will be in the process of trying to bolt. Square your stance so that you have balance, and sharply pull down on the lead twice, saying the command "no." If your horse has any sense, this will startle him into stopping and backing up. Again repeat the command "no," and ask your horse to move forward. He will probably be a little tentative at this point, so encourage him to move forward by clucking and telling him "walk."

The first time you use a chain on your bolting horse, he will be startled into submission—but don't be fooled. He will be thinking of other ways to avoid the chain or to muscle through it. Be careful not to get into a pulling match with him, because he could injure his nose. Instead, always use the chain to bump him off of the lead (pulling down once or twice sharply and then releasing) to prevent him from fighting against the correction. Pay attention to your stance while you work with this horse. He is using a one-thousand-plus-pound frame against your one- or two-hundred-plus-pound body. If you aren't careful, he could pull you right off of your feet. Pay attention to how you are standing and you will be able to position yourself so that he will have a hard time knocking you over. Keep your feet spread and your knees bent, and grip the lead or lunge line firmly.

When on the lunge line, your horse will speed up and duck his head as he attempts to pull away. Usually, he will get up a good head of steam, bunch his back feet underneath himself, and yank his head to the outside. When you see your horse start to speed up, check him back by giving a series of downward jerks on the lunge line and telling him to "trot." If he does not respond immediately, begin shortening the lunge line, bringing your horse close to you and keeping him more under control. As you shorten the line, you decrease his leverage and lessen the amount of lunge line that your signal must pass through to reach him. This also brings his head to the inside, making him shift his weight from back to front and lessening the impulsion from his hind end. All of these tactics work in your favor. Continue bringing him in until he is close enough to reprimand effectively.

Again, give him several sharp tugs of the line and tell him "no." If necessary, bring him to a complete stop to get him under control. Once he is standing quietly, ask him again to "trot," and slowly let him out on the lunge line. Once he is trotting nicely, ask again for the canter. Continue to train him out of this habit until you are sure that he will no longer attempt to bolt, then switch back to a standard lead or lunge line without the chain.

Whenever possible, don't allow these habits to build in the first place. If your horse is young, stay aware of these possibilities and prevent the occasional occurrence of misbehavior from turning into a full-blown habit. Consistency is the key to preventing this long-term behavior. By correcting your young horse quickly and consistently, he will work out of the problem long before he ever gets it ingrained in his head. As soon as he learns that it is more trouble to misbehave than it is to do what he is told, he will shift his efforts elsewhere. Your job is to stay a step ahead of him and to prevent each attempt at mischief from becoming a permanent part of his repertoire.

The Horse That Bucks

Horses begin bucking as a natural response to threat or fear. While running loose, horses buck as a form of play and as a release of energy. Even on the lunge line, bucking can often be the result of an abundance of energy. Bucking under saddle, however, is an entirely different matter and must be stopped quickly before it ever becomes a habit. Under no circumstances should you allow even a crow-hop to pass without a reprimand. Your horse must learn unequivocally that "no bucking" is one of those hard-and-fast rules, regardless of what he is feeling.

Fortunately, even if his bucking does go beyond rambunctiousness, it is one of the few habits that, unless your horse is really good at it, is easy to break. Usually, a few strong reprimands delivered immediately after the behavior will stop this habit cold. Your horse will learn other, more acceptable, ways of venting his anger and frustration, and you must learn to respect and understand these signs and work to help him overcome these obstacles. Realize that your horse is probably using this behavior to tell you that he is uncomfortable about something you are doing. After you break the habit, examine the circumstances and determine what it was that caused your horse to retaliate. You may have to change your training approach in order to teach him effectively. This is *not* to say that you shouldn't teach a certain lesson. Simply find another approach that your horse will respond to positively.

It is particularly easy to predict bucking in a young horse. He has not yet perfected this skill with the added weight of a saddle and a person, and he is therefore easy to dissuade. Watch for the obvious signs of his intentions—when he pins his ears, swishes his tail, hunches his back, and ducks his head—then act accordingly. If he bucks often while he is lunging or at liberty, he will be more prone to bucking when he is under saddle. Watch for these tendencies so that you can be prepared if he chooses this form of rebellion.

It may be more difficult to predict bucking in an older horse, because he has perfected the art and is probably quite good at catching you unaware. You may have few, if any, signs that he is about to buck, and you will have to stay alert and on your toes until you can repeatedly catch him in the act and impose hasty reprimands. If you are caught off guard, do your best to stay seated and retain control of the reins. Gather your reins back up as quickly as possible to gain control and, once he has stopped, reprimand from there.

The first step is to stop your horse in the act. If he bucks only once and then bolts, keep a short rein and pull him around in a tight circle to stop his momentum and bring him to a halt. If he bucks repeatedly, bring his head up and to one side to stop the bucking, then circle him quickly to stop his momentum. Once stopped, use either a spur or a whip to give him two or three hard smacks in the side while telling him "no." Make him turn in a very tight circle for a minute or two, then take him back out on the rail and ask him to perform the requested task. If he tries to buck again, repeat the procedure. It is important that you reprimand him quickly and sharply, but do not let your temper get the best of you. You may be angry, but taking it out on your horse will only be counterproductive. Stay calm and reasonable. Keeping your head and acting only as the situation demands will prevent you from losing control and exacerbating the situation.

Once you learn your horse's "hints" to his intentions, try to stop him from bucking before he actually tries it. Stay aware of his body language (ears, eyes, tail, etc.), and when you sense that he is considering bucking, tell him "no." If he starts to react, immediately pull his head up and to one side in a tight circle, repeating the command "no." After a minute or two, take him back into a straight line. By catching him before he actually bucks, you will begin to make him think twice *before* he acts. This is the training that will eventually solve the problem permanently. Let him know that you are on to him and that he will not get away with acting this way.

In some instances, a horse has been allowed to perfect the art of bucking to the extent that, once he gets started, it is almost impossible for the rider to stay on. He is a master at deception, and you won't realize his intentions until he is in full swing. By then it is too late. This type of horse should be reformed only by a professional. The trainer is better equipped to deal with this animal. A trainer will have several tricks to provoke the behavior and can be prepared to respond. Only then will this bucker be caught in the act while someone still has enough balance to correct the behavior and thus deter it. It is not worth the risk to play the hero and ultimately get hurt. It solves nothing and will only breed resentment and fear between you and your horse. Acknowledge when you are in over your head and seek professional help to solve the problem. It is the only safe, fair way to handle the situation and to create a permanent solution.

The Horse That Rears

Silver was known for his trick rearing in the movies, but unless you are training your horse for a film career, rearing can become a tiresome and dangerous problem—one that is more difficult to break than bucking, and one that can be significantly more dangerous. A horse that is good at rearing has built up his hind end to the point that he can actually spin or jump while in the middle of a rear. Even with a horse that is just beginning this nasty habit, it only takes one time of getting conked by that swinging head to know that you have a serious problem on your hands.

If your horse uses rearing as his way of protesting, he will almost certainly give you clues that rearing is his weapon of choice. You will notice that when he gets frustrated or angry, he may throw his head up and pop his front feet off of the ground a few inches. He may even respond this way after a reprimand or when asked to go someplace that he does not want to go. Reprimand any indication at all, no matter how slight, that he is thinking of getting his front end off of the ground. A sharp smack on the shoulder with a crop and a harsh "no" should start him thinking.

Before you automatically assume that your horse is simply misbehaving, and unless your horse has a history of rearing in the past, check to see if outside factors could be causing the avoidance. First check his teeth. Sharp spurs on the surface of his tooth could make any bit contact in his mouth very painful. He may be rebelling to your demands not out of disobedience but out of pain. By pulling back on the bit, you are altering the position of the bit in his mouth and against his cheeks. If a spur is present, this alteration of position could cause the spur to cut into his cheeks on one or both sides of his mouth. The rearing becomes an escape from pain rather than an avoidance of performance. If you find that this is the case, have your veterinarian file or "float" your horse's teeth to remove these sharp edges.

An ulcerated tooth or gum could also be another painful cause for rearing. While looking for sharp edges, check also that your horse has not banged his gums or teeth on the feeder or bars of the pen. An open sore can be painful when pressure is applied. Hay that has been jammed into the gum or between teeth can be another source of irritation, as can an improperly fitted bit that has caused a rub or an abrasion on the outside of the lips. Be sure to exhaust all of these possibilities before assuming that your horse is just misbehaving.

Another cause of rearing could be the bit. It could be improperly fitted, too harsh for your horse, or inserted incorrectly into his mouth. All of these will cause discomfort to the point that your horse will avoid any and all pressure on his mouth. If the bit is too tight, your horse will experience constant pressure on the sides and roof of his mouth. Any increase in pressure could cause a blowup, and rearing may be his way to escape. A bit that is too narrow will also cause problems. As your horse works, he will be rubbed constantly by the pinching action of the bit. Eventually, he will get fed up with the pain and will rebel.

If the severity of the bit is changed suddenly, you can wreak havoc on your training and create undue stress on your horse. If your horse is accustomed to being worked in a snaffle and you suddenly put a high-port curb in his mouth, you will most certainly be asking for trouble. Always use the least severe bit that you can with your horse without giving up control. If your horse has been ridden with a severe bit in the past (which makes his mouth increasingly hard, causing you to increase the severity of the bit) and you choose not to perpetuate this cycle, try switching to a mechanical hackamore. Most horses respond well to this type of bridle, and it will eliminate the toughening of his mouth. If you are having problems with your horse responding to the bit, work more on training rather than automatically increasing the severity of the bit. While sometimes this may be necessary, most problems can be solved by a change in training methods rather than by a change in bits.

An often overlooked cause of rearing is an improperly inserted bit, most commonly a snaffle. Because of the breaking/flexing action of a snaffle, it is easy to get one upside down or backwards when cleaning a bridle and putting it back together. If it is inserted in your horse's mouth this way, it will totally change the action of the bit and will cause biting and pinching on his gums and cheeks. It will also put extreme, painful pressure on his tongue and the roof of his mouth. While most people will get off and check the adjustment of the bridle itself, an improperly inserted bit may be noticeable only if you take off the entire bridle. If your horse suddenly starts acting up, check all of these possibilities before continuing.

Consider one more outside factor before you decide that you have a problem horse—the use of your hands. When you ask a horse to back or yield to the bit, then raise your hands above the withers and yank back on his mouth, you are asking for rebellion, especially if the horse still has a sensitive mouth that has not been abused in the past. If someone walked up and hit you in the face, wouldn't you react? The extreme action of your hands will have the same effect on your horse. Remember—you are supposed to be training, not forcing, your horse to respond to your commands. If you overreact to the situation, expect your horse to do the same, and don't get mad at him when he does.

So what if you have checked all of these items and you find that you truly have a problem? There are proper and improper ways of reprimanding a horse with a rearing problem. Your first instinct may be to do anything to get your horse's head down, including smacking him on the head. This is not a proper reprimand. As before, hitting your horse's head is never a solution, but limiting his mobility is. While you may be tempted to raise your hands when he begins to rear, force yourself to do just the opposite. Drop your hands to increase your leverage and you will gain more control of his head. It is very hard for him to rear if his nose is tucked in. Turning his head to one side will also control his head and reduce his ability to get his front end off of the ground. By turning his head, you are changing the weight balance on his shoulders, and he cannot effectively get his rear end underneath himself and both feet off of the ground. In both instances, you are using a change in momentum and leverage to prevent the action.

Once you have actually stopped his upward motion, reprimand and correct him to keep him from doing it again. With a crop or a whip, give him two hard smacks on his shoulder, then turn him in a tight circle for a minute, telling him "no." Do not use backing as a means of reprimanding this horse, because you could encourage him to rear again. When you have completed this correction, ask your horse to again move forward. If he starts to go up or plants his feet and refuses to move, repeat the reprimand. Keep working until he walks off freely without protesting, then praise him for performing correctly. You must be vigilant to catch him doing both good and bad things, and consistently respond accordingly. Once again, persistence will win out.

The Horse That Lies Down

The horse that lies down with a saddle or rider on his back, while not as common as a horse that rears or bucks, can be every bit as frustrating to correct. This horse is usually lazy and uses lying down as a sign that he is sick of working and would rather just lie around and relax. While it might be humorous the first time it happens, this behavior gets old quickly. After the amusement dies, you are left with a horse that decides he is the one to set the schedule, and if he doesn't feel like working, he won't. No matter how you look at it, this problem is no laughing matter.

Fortunately, this, too, is fairly easy to solve, but you will need to stay on your toes to avoid getting rolled on. When your horse stops suddenly, or has been standing for a few minutes, pay attention to his body motions. Before a horse lies down, he will either paw the ground, bunch his hind and front feet together, and/or buckle his knees once or twice to adjust his weight. Take any of these motions as an indication that your horse is about to go down. To respond, get your horse moving, either forward, backward, or in a circle. If your horse has already planted his feet and is starting to go down, get off immediately and use a whip or crop to prompt him to stand up again. Once he is up, remount and turn him in a tight circle, telling him "no." After a minute or two, ask him to stand quietly. If he tries to roll again, repeat the procedure.

If at all possible, stay on your horse and get him to respond. Until you can get to this point, you will only be "putting out fires" as they appear. Once you can get him to respond while you are mounted, you will be able to work on long-term prevention of the problem. Be careful not to get trapped or rolled on by your horse if he is indeed going down. If you are confined against a fence or rail and could get trapped, you are better off to dismount than to get hurt. If necessary, enlist the help of a friend to get your horse moving so that you can stay mounted. Have your friend stand behind and off to one side of your horse with a whip in hand, and have him or her smack your horse on the rear whenever he starts to go down. That and your legs (preferably with blunt spurs) should be enough to get him moving again. As always, continue training until he consistently responds appropriately and stands quietly without calling it quits.

Training a Barn-Sour Horse

One of the most frustrating problems is when your horse has bonded so strongly with a pasture or stable mate that you have to deal with World War III when you want to take your horse away by himself. From whinnying and refusing to move, to wheeling and bolting, your horse will pull out all the stops to keep from being separated from his pal, and it may even get to the point where it is so much of a hassle that you stop trying. Don't despair—there is a solution.

First, consider why these bonds form. Your horse is, by nature, a herd animal and is not accustomed to dealing with life out on his own. While many horses seem to have an innate independence, others rely on the comfort and support of their buddies to face day-to-day life. They are the ones that rely on the stronger herd mares to keep them safe and secure from outside threats. They are followers rather than leaders and will never take the lead if they have an opportunity to avoid it. If your horse has a natural tendency to be timid, he may very well fall into this category. While your horse may be in a separate pipe corral rather than in a community pasture, he may still bond with his "neighbors" in order to gain this support.

You will know immediately if your horse has formed this type of bond with one of the neighboring horses. Whenever you remove your horse from his pen, either your horse, the other horse, or both will begin screaming for the return of the buddy. If your horse is the one whinnying, he may also prance along or try to wheel back toward the pipe corral. After you saddle him and are ready to leave the ranch (such as on a trail ride), your horse may plant all four feet and refuse to move. He may balk at a certain point and either spin and try to run back, or dance in place while refusing to move forward. He may even try to rear rather than leave his long-lost friend. The key is to minimize the bond with the other horse while strengthening the bond between yourself and your horse.

Bonds form whenever your horse spends time with either a human or another horse. Like humans, horses are social animals and enjoy spending time around those with whom they are most comfortable. If your horse spends a lot of time in his corral and sees you only on occasion, you are asking for a problem. On the other hand, if you spend a lot of time grooming, working, and just being with your horse, he will come to rely on you as a "stable mate" and will become less dependent on the other horses around him.

If possible, do not ride your horse with his stable mate until the problem is solved. Instead, take him out by himself or with different horses with whom he does not have a bond. Whenever possible, work him out of earshot of the other horse, or at least where they cannot see each other. The more time they spend away from each other, the better. Eventually, you want your horse to rely on you for companionship. The other horses should become immaterial, and he should rely on you for guidance and support. Spending time with him is the only way to develop this bond.

Once you have started working on the problem, tackle the balking issue head-on. While you are mounted and have a crop in your hand, walk your horse away from his buddy and off of the property. If he tries to turn around, turn him back the way he came. In other words, if he tries to turn right, turn him back to the left. If he tries to turn left, turn him back to the right. Always correct the horse against the way in which he wants to go, and keep him facing straight away from the pal. If your horse balks (refuses to go forward), take your crop and smack him two times hard on the rump, telling him "no." Once he has settled, urge him forward again with your legs. If he refuses again, reprimand him again. If you are riding with another horse, have that horse go first to encourage your horse forward.

This battle may take a lot of time to work through, and you will have to be patiently firm in your reprimands. Do not give up and go back to the pen. This will only exacerbate your problem and will decrease any hope of reform. By the same token, losing your temper will only promote a conflict of wills with a no-win situation. Stay calm but strong in your request, and do not give up until your horse goes forward. If all else fails, dismount and walk him forward off of the ranch, then remount when you are farther away. It isn't the ideal solution, but it will begin to teach the point until you are able to deal with the problem while remaining mounted.

If all of this is for naught and your horse still spends all the time away from his buddy screaming for his return, you will need to find some way to separate the horses on a daily basis. Either stable them apart or put their pens far enough away from each other that constant contact does not occur. This solution isn't always convenient or even possible, but it could be your only hope of reforming this horse.

The Follower

Another problem that is somewhat akin to the pouting pals occurs on the trail ride with two or more horses. When one horse decides to either trot or canter ahead, your horse may try to follow. At the least, he may dance and prance until you catch up with the other horse. Worst case, he may try to buck or take the bit in his teeth and take off to catch up, totally ignoring you or your wishes. Neither is a whole lot of fun when you are trying to have a relaxing trail ride.

Again, remember that horses are herd animals. They rely on each other for survival and companionship. Unless you work hard at building a bond with your horse that is based on trust and respect, you will have a hard time convincing him to ignore these instincts and to rely on you for direction. Not only are you asking him to refrain from all of the fun, you are asking him to stay back by himself when he is the most vulnerable. Maintain your patience when you are trying to decrease this horse-to-horse bond and to ultimately break this frustrating habit.

First, avoid adding to the problem. If you constantly allow your horse to run full-out with wild abandon on the trails, he will be much more difficult to restrain than a horse that is kept in check—most of the time anyway. Old habits are even harder to break, so if you are used to galloping wildly on the trails and are suddenly trying to break this habit, you must first rid your horse of the idea that every time you go out on trail, he may run the entire time. Start taking your trail rides slowly, either at a walk or a trot, with only short streaks of cantering. When you do canter, refrain from allowing your horse to go all-out. You are trying to teach him that, even out on the trail, he must listen to you when you ask him to slow down or stop. After you have broken this galloping routine, start working on the buddy problem.

For this training, find a trustworthy friend who has a horse. Get a little way from the ranch and ask your friend to move his or her horse ahead at a faster walk, while you restrain your horse. If your horse starts to pitch a fit, bring him to a stop, and do not allow him to go on until he has quieted down to a walk. If he begins to rear or really react, stop and back up, or turn your horse around so that he is facing away from the other horse. Then make him stand quietly. Once he does this, turn him back around and tell him "walk." Your horse must learn that the only way he will get to go forward is if he walks quietly. If he starts to jig, pull him back to a complete stop, then tell him "walk."

After a short time, your horse should begin to get the idea that if he really pitches a fit, he will have to stop and his buddy will go farther ahead. Once he can deal with your friend's horse walking faster than he is, ask your friend to trot his or her horse away (but not too far), while you keep your horse at a walk. If he starts to throw a tantrum, stop (telling him "whoa," of course) and make him stand until he settles down, then tell him "walk." You may have to work your way through several temper tantrums that will no doubt include jigs, sideways trots, small rears, sneezing, and a multitude of other bratty behaviors. Whatever you do, *don't* give in and allow your horse to hurry and catch up. It will only make matters worse and will reinforce his inappropriate behavior. Let him walk only to catch up (after your friend stops), and restrain him to the speed that you want him to go. Stay calm and quiet, and respond to each tantrum logically and consistently. It is imperative that he know that you will let him catch up to the other horse only when he can proceed at your pace and in your time.

You can also minimize the problem while you work. By making all of your rides carefully controlled training lessons, you will decrease the frustration of both you and your horse. Otherwise, you are bound to catch yourself in a situation where someone decides to take off at a gallop without warning you, and you will have a very upset, out-of-control horse on your hands. All of your previous work will go right down the tubes. Make sure that riding companions know of the work you are doing with your horse and agree to keep you abreast of their intentions before they act. This way, you can prevent any surprises and can control the amount of restraint. Your horse is like a big kid—he can take only so much temptation before he finally gives in. Even the best youngster will act up if pushed too far. Be sensitive to this, and ask him to restrain only at certain times and in certain situations.

This behavior is one of the most difficult to break. It will take days and days of patience and difficult rides. You will be tested like you never were before and will be more than tempted to lose your patience. Be forewarned. If you lose your patience, you lose the battle. Only by staying strong and consistent will you bring about reform in your horse. Don't expect him to become an angel overnight, and he won't disappoint you. It took a long time to form the habit (helped along by a strong dose of instincts), and it will take a long time to break it. Stay patient and keep working.

Appendix: Catalog List

Mail-order catalogs are mentioned throughout the book as an alternate source for purchasing horse supplies. While certainly economical, these catalogs are not always easy to find. Below is a list of some of the catalogs I have found to be particularly useful in my equipment search. Either call or write to them, and they will be happy to send you their recent catalog. You might even mention where you found out about them!

Ball Horse Supply
88 West 6th Avenue
Midvale, UT 84047
(801) 255-2621

Big D's Tack and Vet Supplies
P.O. Box 247
Northfield, OH 44067
1-800-321-2142

Chick's
P.O. Drawer 59
Harrington, DE 19952
1-800-444-2441

Hartmeyer Saddlery
7111 West Bethel Avenue
Muncie, IN 47304
1-800-225-5519

Jeffers General and Equine
   Catalogue
P.O. Box 948
West Plains, MO 65775
1-800-533-3377

Schneider's Saddlery
1609 Golden Gate Plaza
Cleveland, OH 44124
1-800-365-1311

State Line Tack, Inc.
Route 121, P.O. Box 1217
Plaistow, NH 03865-1217
1-800-228-9208

United Vet Equine
14101 West 62nd Street
Eden Prairie, MN 55346
1-800-328-6653 Out of State
1-800-862-6065 In State

Valley Vet Supply
East Highway 36, P.O. Box 504
Marysville, KS 66508-0504
1-800-356-1005

World Champion Horse Equipment
730 Madison Street
Shelbyville, IN 37160
1-800-251-3490

Index